Why Businesses Stop Growing & What You Can Do About It

first edition

Brent Howard, Richard Bernstein & Steve Hackney

Foreword by
PETER MOORES

AFG
PUBLISHING

Why Businesses Stop Growing & What You Can Do About It

Brent Howard, Richard Bernstein & Steve Hackney

Published by:

PUBLISHING

AFG Publishing
Academy For Growth Ltd
Springfield House
Water Lane
Wilmslow
SK9 5BG
United Kingdom

Tel: 0844 448 0640 (UK) +44 1928 508 894 (INT)

Foreword

Success is about having a "Point of Difference"

"If you always do what you always did, then you will always get what you always got."

By Peter Moores
(Former England Cricket Coach and now Head Coach at Lancashire County Cricket Club)

You may be wondering why a cricket coach is writing the foreword to a book on growing businesses...

Well it isn't that I've suddenly decided to change professions, though after spending some time with Steve and Brent their principles apply equally to sport as well as business.

The World is changing at a rate that is staggering and the solutions of yesterday are often not good enough to face the challenges of tomorrow.

In this book, Steve, Brent & Richard have put in place a step-by-step guide to help you through the process of change and come up with innovative ideas that are both simple and practical.

Like all good things their solutions make real sense and for those who are brave enough to take on the challenge of change, the rewards are often significant.

So how does this book connect to sport and what I do for a living?

In sport and most high-end activities, we are all looking for that "point of difference". Something that sets you apart from the rest, while giving you the edge required for success. In sports we have players and coaches looking for all sorts of weird and wonderful ways to find the winning formula, though in truth the gimmicks are always found out.

The pathway to success in sports is to have talented players with the necessary "basics", which they can deliver at pace and adapt to any given situation.

Hence the connection with Steve's background in elite rugby, allied to his experience in the field of marketing. This is combined with the wealth of knowledge that Brent has gained over his years as an accountant and his experience using these principles and methods.

This combination has produced a set of basics for building your business, which will take you through the different stages of growth, coupled with best practice financial management.

Their unique approach takes you into the boardroom, allowing you to compare conventional practice or perceived wisdom against the possibilities of taking the road less travelled. The journey is full of common sense that has evolved through their hours of research and the successful practices they have retained along the way.

I spend a lot of my time challenging the players, the support staff and myself to evaluate our current situation to ensure we are moving with the times, knowing that if you stand still you can get overtaken.

We are always looking to improve while maintaining the solid foundations needed for sustained growth.

This book provides a way forward for those who are willing to embrace a new approach and I am confident that it will give you the "point of difference" that we are all hoping to find.

Preface

A friend (but not a client!) of ours was looking stressed. Business wasn't going well. The downturn in the economy had really impacted his business. The good times had vanished. This new economy was ripping the heart out of his business and, no matter what he tried to do to turn things around, it seemed he always hit a brick wall.

Now, his business is a good business. His work ethic is commendable, but before the recession hit he didn't really have to work hard at getting customers. People came from referrals or recommendations and because he built a reputation for delivering on his promises.

Life and business were good.

But when the economy took a dive, his business suffered because he had no 'push-button' way of generating customers. No way of maximizing sales from existing customers. No real expertise on managing cash flow and profitability. Luckily for him, he still has a relatively loyal customer base but even that is being challenged by cut-price competitors. At the moment his business is like a bucket with a number of small holes in the bottom. It's leaking customers and there's nothing being added in the top to stem the tide and nothing being done (despite his efforts) to block the holes.

It's a precarious position and one that many business owners are facing today.

In essence, this is what this book is all about. It's a blueprint for helping you add more customers into the top of the bucket and for retaining existing customers and at the same time ensuring you maximize profits and maintain a positive cash flow.

As Pete says in his foreword, if you keep doing what you're doing, you'll get what you always got. This book will show you exactly what you need to do to do things differently, to ensure your business not only survives in any economy, but thrives.

Plus, the book sets out to show you why most businesses stop growing. More importantly, we will show you exactly what you can do about it. We will show you how to market and grow your business in a simple, cost-effective and time-efficient manner, and simultaneously provide the financial expertise to help you manage your growth so you can maximize your profits.

You'll notice the book is split into 3 sections...

- SECTION 1: Focuses on why businesses stop growing.

- SECTION 2: Focuses on how to grow your business.

- SECTION 3: Focuses on the management of your business.

The methods we use in this book will apply to every business regardless of the industry, the size of your business or whether you sell business-to-business or business-to-consumer. However, to demonstrate where most 'average' and under-performing businesses are now, and the impact of our methods, we will use two imaginary businesses throughout this book. Let us introduce you to:

Black & Grey Widgets and Rainbow Widgets, are today, identical businesses. Both are two owner businesses operating from offices in the same town. Both have been in business for five years, and have half a dozen staff. Both have found growth difficult in the last couple of years and, while business has slowed, the frustrations and worries are growing. The hopes of the early years are starting to fade. What new business they do get comes mainly from referrals or recommendations, and general marketing is largely avoided as it's seen as ineffective.

They both sell the same 'widget'. The widget they're selling is a substitute for what you sell. It could be products, services, professional services or a restaurant or retail store. In the context of this book and what you're about to learn – it doesn't matter. Everything is completely transferable.

Both businesses have a board meeting today with the objective being...

"Where do we go from here?"

Each chapter of the book addresses each agenda point. The first being – 'Why Has Our Growth Slowed?'. This is where our journey together begins...

Agenda

Section 1: Agenda Item 1

1. Introduction

Just over 8 months ago on a cold frosty morning, the owners of two virtually identical businesses came to the uncomfortable conclusion that their businesses were no longer growing. Or at least not growing at the rate they wanted.

You've already been introduced to these businesses: Black & Grey Widgets and Rainbow Widgets.

They're not alone.

According to the U.S. Small Businesses Administration there are 23 million small businesses across the United States. Many are struggling. Although the recession has of course had an impact and made things tougher for many businesses, it hasn't really had a major effect on company liquidations/bankruptcies.

The table below shows the total company bankruptcies over the last 10 years (data produced by the United States Courts)...

Year	Total
2003	37,548
2004	36,785
2005	31,952
2006	35,292
2007	21,960
2008	30,741
2009	49,091
2010	61,148
2011	54,212
2012	46,393

Why Businesses STOP Growing

The U.S. officially went into recession in the second quarter of 2008 and stayed in recession until the start of 2010 (Bureau Of Economic Analysis). The economy then grew steadily until 2012. While overall, the economy grew in 2012 it shrank in the fourth quarter by 0.1%. 2013 looks no better with predicted growth at less than 1.6%.

As an average, bankruptcies from 2003 to 2007 were 32,707 per year and then when the recession hit, bankruptcies, as you'd expect, jumped to an average of 46,993. That's an increase of 43.7%. Interestingly since 2010 bankruptcies have risen significantly even though the economy was officially growing!

So yes, it gets tougher when the growth in the economy slows – no news there. But what is surprising and shocking is that even when times are good there are still from between 32,000 and 54,000 bankruptcies every year. You can't blame the economy for this!

Of course there are many reasons for the failure of businesses, but almost every one of these can be overcome by getting in more cash. More customers. More sales from existing customers. When you have positive cash flow – you have a sustainable business and most problems disappear.

So, yes you can blame the economy for increased business failures, but ultimately there is no reason to suggest that you can't survive and prosper no matter what the business conditions are.

With little hope of a significant change of fortunes in the coming months, business owners face a challenging time ahead.

A wise man once said, "If you've stopped growing, you're actually shrinking." Nothing is more fundamentally true when it comes to your business. If you're not acquiring new customers then you are almost certainly going backwards.

Even if you are great at servicing customers, you will always lose a small number through the likes of mergers, acquisitions, retirement, bankruptcy (more so at the moment), death, relocation and of course competition.

So, alarmingly, if your business has slowed, it won't be long before it starts going backwards, just like our two case study businesses.

However, the good news is, with the right advice and good old-fashioned hard work, you can buck this trend and create a fast-growing and dominant business. A business that grows month to month.

That's why we wrote this book.

You are reading this book because you see it as the first step in doing something about the growth of your business. We of course don't know your exact personal situation, but we do know you want improvement in your business. And we do know, for whatever reason, you're not happy with things as they stand at the moment. Realizing this, as our two businesses have done, is part of the battle.

Next it's all about what you do about it. You need to get busy and start implementing a range of strategies that will help you...

- Stand out from the crowd
- Attract customers easily
- Remove price from the mind of the customer
- Provide added value that no other competitor can compete with
- Acquire the right type of customers at the right price
- Achieve everything your skills, effort and experience deserve

That's why this book is so important. It's to give you proven solutions to each and every one of these things. But be warned. Although growing your business is down to some basic fundamentals, many of the things we talk to you about will fly in the face of what you believe to be true. You have to trust us. This stuff works. It doesn't matter if you're a sole proprietor or in a business with three or twenty-three partners. But to get results, you have to change what you're doing. You have to be different. You cannot hope to achieve all you want with an attitude of 'this will never work for my business'. You have to open your mind to the opportunities that present themselves to you in this book. And if you do, then you're going to enjoy the results of your efforts. We promise you that.

So let's get started. We've given you full access to each partner meeting. Black & Grey Widgets are going it alone. Rainbow Widgets have invited us to help them.

Enjoy the journey...

2. Why Has Our Growth Slowed?

Introduction

To understand why growth slows or stagnates in any business, we first need to look at how a typical business evolves and why the frustration starts to mount as this growth slows. We call this the 'Growth Roller-Coaster'.

Take a look at the illustration below.

The Growth Roller-Coaster

The starting point is the beginning of the business, usually created by an individual or a small number of partners. Typically, the owners are very hands-on at this stage with few, if any, staff and modest resources. In the early months and years the business grows very well.

Customers receive a high degree of attention with good levels of customer service as a result. Costs in the modest operation are relatively low and the business can respond quickly to customer and market needs.

Word is spread by customers and referrers and new business is easily gained. The business expands to a peak at point **A**, driven by the personalities and skills of its owners.

In an ideal world, two conditions will now be met. Firstly, the owners will recognize that they have reached the pinnacle for a personality-driven business, and secondly, the business and financial performance will be at a level that completely satisfies them. In reality, neither is the case.

What happens in the real world is that the owners continue to drive forward. However, with the growth there now come problems...

Staff and resource levels have been increased to serve the growing customer base, increasing costs and tying up owner time. Owners themselves come under increasing time pressure, being torn between customers, staff and running the business. Falling service levels and rising costs see the growth constricted and dissatisfaction around the business grows in its place.

Have you ever heard yourself or a colleague say, "This was so much easier in the early days!"

Now the owners find themselves at point **C**. Right now, you are likely to be at some point between **A** and **C**.

Reality has dawned and the business is at a crossroads. Do you remain a personality-driven business and attempt to claw your way back to point **A** by downsizing and try to raise point A to a higher pinnacle? Or do you undertake the investment (mostly in time and effort) required to move forward to become a systems-based business at point **C?** Since you're reading this book it's highly likely this is what you want to achieve.

Interestingly, both types of business can be successful with the right planning and management. However, too many businesses find themselves falling into the trough in between, simply because they've not considered early enough what their fundamental strategies and goals will be. So much emphasis is placed upon the process function, delivering the product or service to customers, that the essential marketing and financial management of the business itself is overlooked. Growth, consequently, is flawed.

Let's look then at the high-level view of your business (any business). As we mentioned above, it has three key components...

1. **Process**
   The mechanics by which a business 'produces' its saleable products or services and delivers them to its customers. This is how you generate your income.

2. **Marketing**
   The generation of new customers, the retention of existing customers and the maximization of customer value. This is how you acquire and retain your customers.

3. **Management**
   The running of the business – its financial performance, strategies, administration and goals. This is how you generate profit and wealth.

Let's take a closer look at what this looks like...

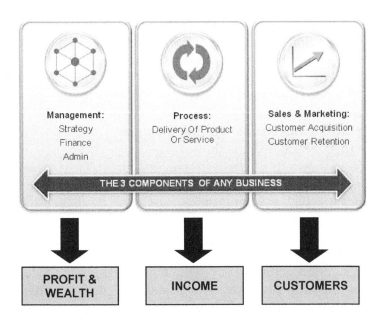

When a business is growing steadily and reaching the owners' objectives, the 3 functions work together to create a harmonious cycle...

- **PROCESS:** Delivery of the product or service to customers is profitable and delivered beyond expectation.

- **MARKETING:** New customers are won and retained.

- **MANAGEMENT:** The business is managed smoothly at all levels.

In reality, the majority of people are taught process skills from school days, through studies and onwards. We are taught how to read and write. How to do math and answer questions.

You develop expertise in how to 'do things'. You ultimately learn how to create and deliver your product or service to your customers.

In other words, your expertise and skills invariably lie in the **PROCESS** function. Consequently, with the skills and knowledge loaded towards the process function, businesses can only grow while there is capacity within the process function to do so.

But **without** the same relative development in the management and, in particular, marketing functions, **growth and profitability become limited**...

The cycle now starts to look very different...

- **PROCESS:** Delivery of the product or service becomes hit or miss. Service levels drop. Complaints grow.

- **MARKETING:** Becomes neglected and ineffective. Any customer gains are offset by customer losses.

- **MANAGEMENT:** Customers are frustrated, causing more work. Staff and processes are inefficient. Cash flow becomes harder to manage and profits drop.

So the solution is simple...

You need to start putting more effort into the marketing and management functions of the business to realign the balance.

This doesn't mean you neglect the process function. It just means you work smarter and allocate your time and effort better to include these two crucial areas of your business.

So, there is little doubt as to why most businesses do not achieve the growth objectives the owners have set, and why now is the time to make the transition from a process-led business to a management-led, and in particular, a marketing-led business.

Our goal is for you to have a systems-based business that is set up to achieve your objectives. The rest of this first section shows you how to achieve growth through a series of proven sales and marketing strategies that you can automate. Section 2 focuses on the management side of the business, and in particular the financial management of the business.

Black & Grey Widgets

Of course Black & Grey know their growth has slowed, but they blamed it on the economy. There's no need to panic. It's tough for everyone. Things will turn around and they've not lost that many customers... yet. Yes, as we saw earlier, the economy has played a part, but only a small part. The big reason for its slowdown is how the business is marketed.

Black & Grey, in fairness, know they're not doing enough marketing. So on the basis of 'we need to do more marketing', they move on to agenda item 3.

Rainbow Widgets

"So you see, you've reached point C on the 'Growth Roller-Coaster', that's why your business has slowed in its growth. Now you understand why this has happened, you're in a much better position to do something about it.

"What we want to make clear is you have absolutely no control over outside forces such as the economy, the competition, and low-price competition. You can only control what you do and by taking control you can minimize and virtually eliminate the effect of these non-controllable market forces.

"So now you have a good grasp of why the business has slowed in its growth, let's look at how you can grow the business."

Key Summary & Action Points

1. Re-read this section to fully understand why your business has stopped growing (or slowed down).

2. Take responsibility for the position your business is in. You cannot and must not blame anything

outside your control. You (and any other owners) are and must be the only people who can drive your business forward.

3. Understand that as long as you have the right attitude (this WILL work for me rather than this will never work in my business) then no matter where your business is on the Growth Roller-Coaster you can take steps to overcome any challenge you have by implementing the advice in this book.

2. Why Has Our Growth Slowed?

3. How Do We Grow Our Business?

Introduction

The good news is that growing any business comes down to some sound basic fundamentals, some of which you will have been exposed to before and others you won't.

Now remember, our goal is to help you create a system-led business on autopilot, so the growth of the business has to be based around an easy-to-apply marketing system.

We'll show you the system first, and then we can explain it in more detail. Here's what your system should look like (see next page).

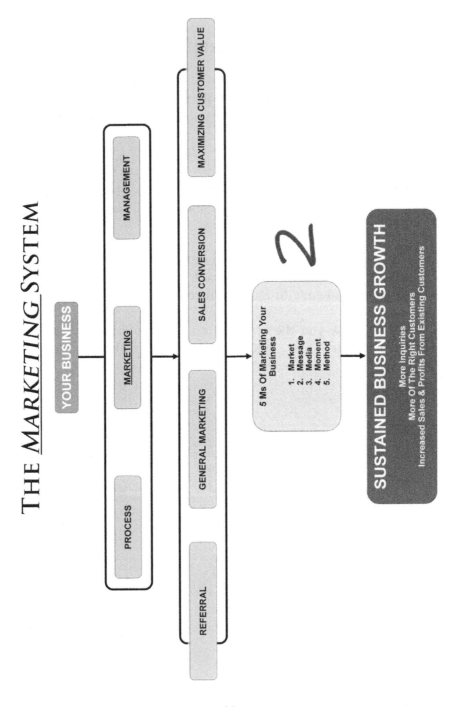

THE *MARKETING* SYSTEM

YOUR BUSINESS

PROCESS | MARKETING | MANAGEMENT

REFERRAL | GENERAL MARKETING | SALES CONVERSION | MAXIMIZING CUSTOMER VALUE

5 Ms Of Marketing Your Business
1. Market
2. Message
3. Media
4. Moment
5. Method

SUSTAINED BUSINESS GROWTH
More Inquiries
More Of The Right Customers
Increased Sales & Profits From Existing Customers

As you can see, there are actually just two 'levels' to a powerful marketing system and when they're combined you create a business that keeps growing and growing. Let's take a closer look at each level...

1. **'The 4 Business Multipliers' (4 Ways To Grow Your Business):**

    Other than buying other businesses, there are just 4 ways to grow your own business...

    *   <u>Referral:</u> We all know that generating inquiries by referral is THE single best way to get customers. However, virtually every business has what we call a 'reactive referral process' in place. <u>This ISN'T a system</u>. This 'ad hoc' approach will only get you so far, but when you want to achieve growth targets, you cannot hope to grow your business on this basis. The key word in all of this (which you'll hear a lot from us) is **SYSTEM**. Systemizing your referrals from customers and other third-party referral sources is key to your success.

    *   <u>General Marketing:</u> Rigorous testing has provided us with a number of proven marketing approaches which enable businesses to generate many inquiries at will. The reason why most businesses believe that general marketing is often ineffective is explained in (2) below.

        However, a critical piece of the success jigsaw is to use a number of marketing approaches, not just one or two (another key reason why most businesses don't grow at the rate they should).

        We have a saying: "Other than zero, the worst number in business is '1'; 1 key customer, 1 key supplier, 1 key employee and 1 marketing approach." You are seriously harming your business if you only use one or two marketing approaches (another big cause of growth slowing).

- Sales Conversion: When your referral and general marketing systems are operating effectively, they will generate a healthy supply of inquiries every month. As soon as an inquiry is generated, your 'sales conversion system' should kick in.

  In other words, you should have a system in place that helps the prospective customer through your sales process, ensuring they become a customer.

  You need to build in a number of stages, whereby each one moves the prospective customer closer to the sale. Once again this is a BIG weakness we see in most businesses – there isn't usually any kind of sales conversion system in place.

  We have come across businesses that were only converting 1 in 10 inquiries (from general marketing inquiries) prior to implementing a sales conversion system. Take note that we are talking about true conversion rates here. Many businesses kid themselves that their conversion rates are higher than they actually are because they only count the 'easy' pickings from warm referrals and ignore all the failed general marketing efforts. Once the system was in place, they improved their conversion to between 7 and 9 out of 10.

  This makes a huge difference to your new customer acquisitions – and is achieved with absolutely ZERO extra cost.

- Maximizing Customer Value: Much has been written and spoken about selling more products or services to existing customers. In reality, many businesses find this one of their most challenging tasks. But it needn't (and definitely shouldn't) be so. The reality is that most businesses just miss so many golden opportunities to up-sell and cross-sell their products or services, again because no formal system is in place for actually doing it.

You know as well as we do that little thought is ever given to putting in place a solid system that identifies the opportunities for selling more products or services to customers, and what exactly has to be done when these opportunities arise.

> **IMPORTANT NOTE:**
>
> As you can imagine, just small improvements across each of the 4 Business Multipliers will result in big increases in growth. That's the power of the business multipliers.

2. The 5 Ms Of Marketing Your Business:

So you know that there are 4 ways to grow your business. However, this still isn't enough. Each of these methods must be underpinned by a set of time-tested rules which ensure their success. We call these the '5 Ms of Marketing Your Business' (Market, Message, Media, Moment and Method)...

- Market: Who you are targeting (your 'Target Market').

- Message: Why someone should use your business rather than anyone else (your competitors) and what you need to convey in your message to get people to respond and buy.

- Media: The marketing channels you will use to deliver your message to the market (i.e. website, advertisements, direct mail, articles, etc.).

Why Businesses Stop Growing...

- <u>Moment:</u> Timing is everything!

- <u>Method:</u> What 'marketing piece' will you use for each media, to rise above the clutter and get noticed over EVERY other business that's marketing to your target market (notice these are your direct competitors AND every other type of business trying to get your potential customers to buy from them).

So there you have it. That's what it takes to grow any business – no matter where you are in your evolution. No matter how long you've been established. No matter what your goals and objectives are. This is the system that will bring you the results you need.

Black & Grey Widgets

Like most businesses, Black & Grey doesn't utilize all 4 of the Business Growth Multipliers, nor do they understand or appreciate why the 5 Ms Of Marketing Your Business play such an important part in acquiring and retaining the right customers.

This ignorance and lack of knowledge means they will never reach their potential. Worse still, it could mean that everything they try to implement from this day forward simply won't work (or work as well as it should)!

They complete this part of the meeting by agreeing that they need to do more 'marketing' (which means they are going to focus on how to generate more inquiries).

However, and thankfully, they recognize the need to at least try and target the right people for their business.

Rainbow Widgets

"We said none of this was rocket science. Now you've seen the marketing system and you understand the basics of each element, hopefully you can see that its success lies in its simplicity.

"But we guarantee as long as you apply each element to your business, you will see the growth that you seek.

"However, the scale of your success depends on how well you execute each of the elements in the system. So let's take a look at the first and most important part of growing your business – the target market."

Key Summary & Action Points

1. Re-read this section to fully understand the two key components of your business growth system.

2. Understand that for your business to grow and dominate your competition, you need a marketing system that runs on autopilot.

3. Appreciate that improving every component by just a small fraction will have a big overall impact on your business as a whole.

Why Businesses Stop Growing...

4. How Do We Acquire The Right Customers For Us?

Introduction

To get the best possible results from each of the Business Growth Multipliers and all the marketing pieces you use, you must first, and most importantly, clearly identify the type(s) of customers you are looking to target. These are known as 'target markets'.

The ideal Target Market is a clearly identified group(s) of people/organizations who/which...

1. Need – and more accurately 'want' – your products or services

2. Can afford to pay for your products or services

3. Can be easily reached by your marketing efforts

4. Have similarities (demographic/psychographic) that enable you to 'group' them together

---

One of the biggest mistakes you can make is to try and be 'all things to all people'. Yes, there is success to be found using this approach, but by focusing on one or more carefully chosen 'target markets' you'll be far more successful, and this success will be achieved much quicker than with any other approach.

So why do so many businesses try to be all things to all people? In most cases it's because they're frightened to 'limit' the number of potential customers they specifically target.

They think if they reduce the number of prospects, they'll risk their whole livelihood!

Nothing could be further from the truth. Let us explain...

We're often asked – "If I limit my market, won't I be reducing the chances of doing business with more people?"

Yes you will. But to succeed in today's competitive market place, you need to concentrate your marketing on a small number of well-chosen target markets, into which you pour all of your resources.

Of course, if you focus on a smaller group(s) you may miss the business from outside the target group. But what actually happens is you increase the amount of business you receive from the target group.

This is because you are specifically meeting the target market's needs and requirements. You are saying to them that you are THE business who knows about their situation – their wants and desires – their problems – and their concerns. No other business specifically meets their needs in this way and therefore the business is seen as the logical company to turn to.

So you must define who your target market is BEFORE you do anything else.

Traditional Mass Marketing Versus Target Or Niche Marketing...

The diagram on the next page shows the differences between conventional marketing (mass marketing) and 'world-class' marketing that we adhere to (target marketing)...

4. How Do We Acquire The Right Customers For Us?

The Mass Marketing Approach

The Market Universe

The prospects who <u>could</u> buy your products or services – 'Mass Market'.

Prospects Who Are Unlikely To Buy

The white space represents potential customers that are unlikely to buy, but they all receive the same marketing message from the business, which results in needless and excessive expense.

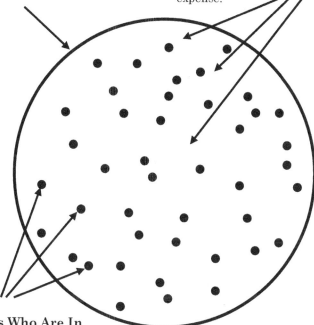

Prospects Who Are In A Position To Buy

Note how disparate these are. The white space in between represents everyone else in the mass market. You have to spend much more money to get 'lucky' and hit the right people/businesses.

The Result

High cost to reach buyers. Response and acquisitions are low because you're targeting everyone with a 'mass market' message – i.e. it doesn't directly appeal to the buyers. Greater effort (on your part!) required to qualify out bad prospects – if you're targeting everyone, you'll also get a large number of poor prospects and YOU DON'T WANT THAT!

Why Businesses Stop Growing...

The Target Market Approach

The Market Universe

The prospects who <u>could</u> buy your products or services – 'Mass Market'.

Prospects Who Are Unlikely To Buy

The white space represents potential customers who are still unlikely to buy, but they all receive the tailored marketing message from you once the inquiry has been generated by your marketing efforts. Notice there are fewer now!

Target or Niche Market
(a smaller segment of the Market Universe)

Prospects Who Are In A Position To Buy

See, now that by concentrating your efforts on a carefully selected target market, you 'capture' a high proportion of potential buyers. Plus, once you've generated the inquiry, your message then also needs to be completely focused on this group so customer acquisitions are increased significantly.

People/Businesses Who Are In A Position To Buy <u>Outside</u> The Target Market

Even this approach isn't perfect – but it's close! You can't hope to 'catch' everyone. There will still be other people/businesses outside the chosen target market(s) that you 'miss'. But notice how few there are.

The Result

This gives you the ability to concentrate your efforts on a more targeted group. Target marketing increases the likelihood of a sale. And enables YOU to take a big slice of this target market.

Multiple Target Markets

You don't have to restrict yourself to just one target market. You may find it necessary to focus on two or more target markets depending on the products or services you provide. For example, an accountant may have three target markets...

- Primary - Start-up businesses
- Secondary - $1 to $2m businesses
- Tertiary - $2m - $5m businesses

...or even more 'vertical' (more defined target markets)...

- Primary - Dentists
- Secondary - Media companies
- Tertiary - Legal

The accountant in this example would need to 'speak' and 'communicate' very differently to each target market once the inquiry has been generated, because they are so different. An accountant cannot speak the same way to a start-up business as you would a $5m business – so why do people do it?

Here's a diagram showing how this looks...

Why Businesses Stop Growing...

Multiple Target Markets

SECONDARY
Target Market

The Market Universe

The prospects who <u>could</u> buy
your products or services –
'Mass Market'.

PRIMARY
Target
Market

TERTIARY
Target Market

The Result

This gives you the ability to concentrate your
efforts on more targeted groups. Target
marketing increases the likelihood of a sale.
And enables YOU to take a big slice of this
target market.

4. How Do We Acquire The Right Customers For Us?

The Power Of Target Marketing

Here's a simple but very powerful example of why defining your target market or niche is so important...

Let's say a start-up business needs an accountant. Their first choice is to perhaps look in the Yellow Pages under the 'Accounting' category. Although there are a number of ads, the first one reads...

> 'ABC Certified Public Accountants. Tax preparation, auditing, bookkeeping, payroll services, help for start-ups, management accounts, and so on.'

The second ad reads...

> 'XYZ Certified Public Accountants. Specializing in helping start-ups get their businesses running quickly, profitably and effectively.'

Which business of accountants are they likely to choose? The answer is obvious. If you can create this bond between your business and the target market(s), we guarantee you'll grow your business quicker than you could ever imagine.

So how do you target the best types of customers? Well, we've created a very simple diagram showing the key characteristics you should look for (note there are two diagrams – first for business-to-business and second for business-to-consumer)...

The Business-To-Business
Target Market Characteristics

Here's a more in-depth look at each characteristic...

- Industry:

    What types of businesses do you want to target? Are there some industries that you want to stay clear of? Do you have any specialties with certain industries? Do you have credibility in any industries?

    There are three key factors which influence the selection of the industry...

    1. Your industry experience

        You may want to target industries where you already have experience.

    2. Your industry credibility

        You may want to target industries where you already have credibility.

    3. Your likes and dislikes

        You may have preferences already about industries that you like or dislike. This will obviously have an impact on the choices you make in terms of the industries you select.

- Decision Makers:

    An important consideration is choosing businesses with a simple decision-making process. Clearly, the larger the business, the more likely the number of decision-makers will increase, making the sale more difficult.

- Age Of Business:

4. How Do We Acquire The Right Customers For Us?

Clearly there is an age range of businesses from start-ups to well-established companies. Are you bothered about how old a business is?

- Revenue / Number Of Employees:

    Both these demographics are easy indicators for choosing your target market.

    Revenue has a direct impact on the number of decision-makers.

    The Number Of Employees is generally linked to revenue and again the greater numbers of staff the larger the company is likely to be. It brings in the decision about working with sole proprietors or not!

- Location:

    Where exactly do you want your customers to come from? Do not ignore those on your doorstep (a common mistake), as long as they fit in with the other characteristics.

- Profitability:

    How concerned are you about working with profitable companies?

Now let's take a look at the business-to-consumer target market characteristics...

The Business-To-Consumer
Target Market Characteristics

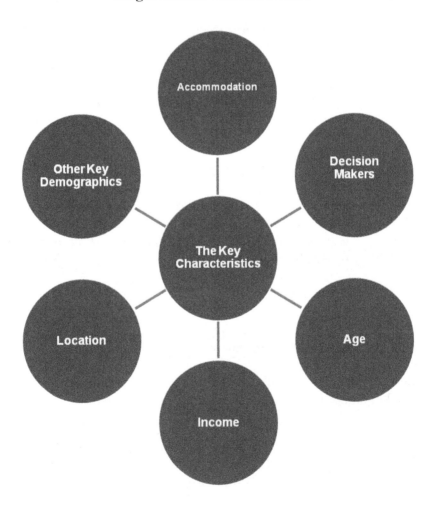

4. How Do We Acquire The Right Customers For Us?

Here's a more in-depth look at each characteristic...

- Accommodation:

  This refers to the type of dwelling your target market lives in. For example, do most of your customers live in 4- or 5-bed detached homes or 3-bed semi-detached? Do they live in apartments or condominiums? Do they have large or small gardens, or none at all?

- Decision Makers:

  Is the male or female the main decision-maker or is it a joint decision (rarely is this the case!).

- Age:

  How old are your typical customers? Does it vary depending on gender?

- Income:

  What is the combined income of the household? If you're selling high-ticket products or services, this will have a significant bearing on your targeting.

- Location:

  Again, where exactly do you want your customers to come from? Do not ignore those on your doorstep (a common mistake), as long as they fit in with the other characteristics.

- Other Key Demographics:

  Depending on the type of product or service you sell, there are a multitude of other key demographics that you would want to consider. For example...

  - Number of children
  - Age of children
  - Schools children go to
  - Type of employment
  - Credit history
  - Type of vehicles driven
  - Number of credit cards held
  - Religion
  - And on and on

  You will know what demographics are important to you. Just make sure you factor them in when identifying what the ideal customer 'looks like'.

Black & Grey Widgets

This is not a time to rush into making knee-jerk and quick decisions about who is the right type of customer. Unfortunately Black & Grey do just that.

Of course they have an appreciation of some of the characteristics (namely, size and location), but this is where the biggest mistakes are made.

You see, they fall into the same trap as 80% of other businesses and decide that they are going after the types of customers they 'wish' they could work with. After all, they have a dozen or so customers like this and they want more.

But if they'd only spent more time on this, they'd have researched their existing customer base and realized that the majority of their business customers, which generate 70% of their sales and profits – don't fit this profile. Yet these are their 'bread and butter' customers. Whether they like it or not, these are the businesses that they are good at working with. These are the customers that, for whatever reason, they are good at acquiring and servicing. These are their low-hanging fruit.

They would also know, if they took the time to analyze, that the average annual income from each of these customers, even though it could be improved (see later), is still a healthy $1,750. Now they may argue that these aren't the 'perfect' customers for them, but if that's the case, they should create another target market out of their 'wish' list customers and then they minimize their risk and maximize potential gains.

Rainbow Widgets

"Do you see, by using the Target Market Characteristics and carefully analyzing your existing customers, how you can pinpoint with a fair degree of accuracy who your best target markets are?

"Our philosophy is clear: it's far less risky to go after the low-hanging fruit as you steadily build your business. This way you get the best of both worlds: steady growth and the eventual acquisition of the customers you really want.

"Of course, before you nail your target market you need to analyze your existing customer base. We don't need to make this decision today. So here's what you need to do."

Key Summary & Action Points

1. Defining your target market is THE most important thing you can do to grow your business.

2. Your target market should represent the 'low-hanging fruit' (easy to acquire).

---

3. If there are two or more target markets that you want to go after, this is fine – but remember these groups ARE different so they will need different messages (see next agenda item).

---

5. How Do We Get People Interested In, Even Excited By Our Products/Services?

Introduction

Having identified your target market, you now need to create the message that you are going to deliver to the market.

This isn't a particularly strong area for many businesses. Our experience tells us that most people really struggle when it comes to creating a powerful message. **THIS IS CERTAINLY A MAJOR REASON WHY MOST MARKETING FAILS**.

Therefore, we will give you a clear insight into why it is so important to create the right message and how to do it.

During the last 20 years or so we've discovered there are a number of crucial elements to a marketing message that, when used correctly, GUARANTEE success.

We call these elements **'Marketing Assets'**. They are the things that ensure you get a response to your marketing pieces.

So let's take a look at each of the Marketing Assets...

The Marketing Assets

1	Gaining Competitive Advantage: Unique Perceived Benefit
2	Adding Sizzle To The Steak: Features Into Benefits
3	Irresistible Offers
4	Headlines
5	Guarantees/Risk Reversal
6	Sales Barrier Demolition Strategy
7	Reasons Why
8	Social Proof
9	Call To Action

1. Gaining Competitive Advantage: Unique Perceived Benefit

A Unique Perceived Benefit (UPB) is the one thing that sets you apart from the competition. Communicating this uniqueness is a powerful and persuasive part of each marketing piece.

This is a very weak area for almost every business and one which really hinders growth.

The problem is that customers (as we said earlier) have become more discerning, which means they're looking for reasons to change or simply use another business – unique reasons; competitive advantages; things that are desirable to them that no other business can offer them.

But because so few businesses create this uniqueness, most people (rightly or wrongly) think ALL businesses are the same within each industry. So, for example, they think all accountants are the same. All printers are the same. All furniture stores are the same. And so on. Changing, for the sake of changing, to another supplier who is just going to be like the existing one, just isn't worth the hassle.

We have therefore identified 10 proven and powerful different UPB categories. You will be able to choose at least one of them for your business...

1. New and Unique

Sometimes you can provide a product or service that's so new and unique that the product or service itself is the UPB. Being the original or first mover in the market is a UPB that nobody can duplicate.

Inevitably, a competitor will emerge with a knock-off or copy of your product or service but, until then, you can promote the newness and uniqueness of your product or service as the UPB.

When the competition heats up, you can switch your UPB so that it positions your business as the 'first' or 'original' one of its kind.

At first, it can appear impossible to come up with something new in your specific industry, but this is about coming up with something new and unique that your customers really want or even dream of having. Think laterally.

2. Highest Quality

One well-known brand that immediately comes to mind when you think about quality is the leading international watch-maker, Rolex. Rolex has a short UPB statement that communicates volumes...

Rolex – "Quality Takes Time"

Rolex have educated the market as to what quality actually means in the context of a watch, and the same is required for customers when it comes to understanding

37

what a 'quality' business is in your industry. Case studies and testimonials are key and we cover these later.

3. Expert Status

This type of UPB communicates the idea that "I/We am/are the top in my/our field. You can trust my/our knowledge and experience".

This works very well for any business, but particularly service-based businesses because it can be firmly focused on the target market you have identified.

4. Amazing Customer Service

Providing superior customer service is a wonderful way to add value, as well as develop long-term customer loyalty.

To surpass the competition you must go beyond simply satisfying customers, you have to AMAZE them. Steve Jobs of Apple Computer built his company around this philosophy.

One of the ways to do this is by using 'Moments Of Truth' (covered later) whereby you look at every point of contact with your customers and create a WOW experience at each point. Just think how many times, and in how many different contexts, your business meets, writes to and telephones customers. This is a huge opportunity going to waste in most businesses, not only to impress the customer, but to give the customer a much better understanding of the true value of the service that they receive.

5. The Largest Size/Selection

Providing the largest selection of items can be a powerfully effective UPB. The classic example of this is Amazon.com. For years (prior to extending their product line) Amazon's UPB was "Earth's Biggest Bookstore".

Even though they were not the first and today they have intense competition, from both online and brick-and-mortar bookstores such as Barnes and Noble and Waterstones, Amazon.com still leads the pack in online bookselling. This is because they clearly differentiated themselves early on by being the biggest.

Most businesses are regularly guilty of not communicating to their customers everything that they do. The businesses that do this well differentiate themselves as well as sell more.

6. Speed

The speed at which your product or service is delivered can be a powerful UPB.

For example, Regus, the serviced office specialists, have a very powerful 3-word UPB that sums up their uniqueness perfectly (quick and everywhere)…

"Instant Offices Worldwide"

FedEx changed the shipping world when it began guaranteeing overnight delivery of packages. Their UPB has stood the test of time…

FedEx – "When It Absolutely Has To Be There Overnight"

What can you do that's faster than your competition?

7. Strongest Guarantee/Risk Reversal/Sales Barrier Demolition

A powerful guarantee/risk reversal/sales barrier demolition can immediately give you a compelling UPB.

Craftsman Tools is a prime example of this UPB category. Like all carefully crafted UPBs, the Craftsman statement leaves you in no doubt as to what their main advantage is...

Craftsman Tools – "Hand tools so tough, they're guaranteed forever"

We are massive advocates of guarantees. The key is therefore to find ones that are meaningful and stand out in your market place. What is it that will reassure your target market?

8. Problem/Solution

Understand that you are not selling a product or service, you're selling a major solution to your target market's most pressing problem(s). Think about the following situation...

You're out for a business lunch and someone you've been speaking to asks you this very familiar question...

> "What do you do for a living?"

Now, when the same question is put to you, you probably answer in this way...

"I'm a <insert your industry>"

This is a very common reply and most people will 'switch off' after asking this question and hearing that reply!

What you must realize is that when you answer in this way regarding your own business, you're saying what you ARE, rather than what you DO FOR YOUR CUSTOMERS!

There's a massive difference.

The good news is your competition ALSO answer in this way – they don't have a UPB. All they are selling is the 'product' or the 'service' and not the result!

To show you what we mean, let's take two common examples and add a UPB...

> Lawyer – "I help people separate within 12 weeks and as amicably as possible"
>
> Printer – "I help people sell more of their products or services using innovative and cost-effective printed materials"

In essence, your UPB completely focuses on what you do for your specific target market(s) or niche(s). It is the major benefit to them – the result of using your services.

By focusing on the customer's most pressing problems you can uncover the major benefit.

Think about your prospects' and customers' fears, obstacles and problems. How does your service reduce or eliminate these fears? For example, a telemarketing service company would say the major problem their prospects and customers have is...

They can't generate enough leads or inquiries themselves.

Here's how you'd then turn this problem into a powerful benefit...

Problem: They can't generate any leads or inquiries.

Benefit: We help businesses generate high-quality leads.

Do you see how easy this is?

So having identified the major problem your product or service solves for your chosen target market(s), write the corresponding benefit down.

If you've identified two or more target markets, it is highly likely you will have one UPB for each target market (which are likely to be different from each other).

9. Magic Wand

If you could wave a magic wand and give your customers and target market(s) one wish, what would they want most? Some of the greatest businesses in the world were founded on such thinking. For example, Microsoft was built on this premise...

> "to make the computer accessible and easy-to-use
> for everyone"

In an inexpensive way, can you reposition your basic offer in order to meet the target market's major need?

10. THE Biggest, Most Important Benefit

This final method is relatively simple. You need to identify every single feature of your product or service, together with how you operate as a business and how you interact with your customers. Having written them down, you then need to convert each of these features into benefits (see the next section on how to do this).

Once you have your list of benefits, you then need to put them in order, with the most potent one at the top. If this is powerful then the major benefit of the product or service will be the UPB.

A good example of this is the 'Tech-ni-fold Tri-Creaser'. The major benefit of the Tri-creaser is that it 'totally eliminates fiber-cracking'. This benefit on its own is so powerful it became the UPB. It was further strengthened by adding the word 'guaranteed' to it...

"Totally Eliminates Fiber-Cracking – Guaranteed"

Now to you and us this means very little, but to printers and print finishers this means everything!

A VERY IMPORTANT NOTE ABOUT USING THE LOWEST PRICE AS THE UPB –

NEVER, EVER DO IT

Guaranteeing the lowest price has been used as a UPB for many businesses in virtually every industry. Right now, as the economy struggles to recover, many more businesses are trying to 'buy' customers.

However, cutting profit margins too deeply is rarely healthy for a business. So, unfortunately, many who have chosen low price for a UPB are no longer in business or are struggling to make ends meet. The philosophy is low margins, but high volume. This is a very difficult model to adopt successfully for most businesses.

We NEVER recommend setting your prices to be the cheapest. There is always someone who will undercut you.

---

2. Adding Sizzle To The Steak: Features Into Benefits

A 'Feature' is a statement of what you do or what something does. It has limited value as it doesn't communicate the 'what's in it for me' factor that all buyers are looking for.

A 'Benefit' is the opposite of a feature. It communicates the end result that the buyer could expect to receive, i.e. something they get rather than something you do. It's amazing how many marketing pieces we see with more features than benefits.

3. Irresistible Offers

This is the part of your marketing that makes someone choose to take action or not. In other words, the offer is what the customer actually gets when they buy from you. An irresistible offer can transform the success of a marketing campaign.

Any offer can be improved by using the following 'Offer Equation'...

Great Offer = Irresistible Promotion + Stimulator (getting people to act now, i.e. a deadline, limited availability, etc.).

4. Headline

A marketing piece without a headline is a mistake made by 95% of businesses, and yet the headline is the 'ad for the ad'. Your business name, for example, is NOT a headline.

Unfortunately people don't care about the name of your business – all they care about is what you can do for them. The headline is the one thing that grabs their attention. Like all of these Marketing Assets, a powerful headline is absolutely compulsory!

5. Guarantee

As we highlighted above when discussing UPB, a guarantee is a proven way to reduce 'buyer hurdles' and is therefore a 'sales converter'. In other words, by offering a guarantee, you eliminate doubts in the mind of the potential customer, resulting in more new customers.

Guaranteeing things like the quality of your goods, work completed on time, response times, and so on can make a huge difference to you.

6. Sales Barrier Demolition

This takes the concept of guarantees to another level. By focusing on the fears and frustrations your customers have with your industry as a whole, you can create a multi-step guarantee (Sales Barrier Demolition) which completely obliterates any buyer

hurdles, significantly increasing sales.

7. Reasons Why

When you have an irresistible offer and a guarantee, you must use 'Reasons Why' to explain why you're offering these things. This ensures the potential customer believes your claims and further increases new customer acquisitions.

8. Social Proof

Social Proof is a combination of assets which help prove your credentials, resulting in more sales. Here's a list of the things we class as Social Proof ...

- Quotes/testimonials from happy customers

- Awards of any kind

- Membership of credible associations ('credible' in the mind of the prospect/customer)

- Review quotes from other media sources

- Quotes from business partners

- Any mention of a joint venture with a well-known brand

- Singing your praises from the rooftops (or more conveniently in areas where customers visit – showroom, office, reception, etc.) is a good thing and an easy opportunity for most businesses. Yet it's missed time and time again.

9. Call To Action

This is an essential part of the marketing piece and a critical Marketing Asset.

The 'Call To Action' needs to give the reader a reason to ACT NOW, e.g. a FREE phone number is not a call to action, a reduced price for responding by a certain date, is. Ideally it should (1) summarize the offer, (2) remind them of the 'stimulator' – a reason to respond now, (3) give them multiple ways of responding and (4) tell them what will happen when they respond/buy.

Black & Grey Widgets

Getting the message right is a significant weakness for Black & Grey. Lack of expertise in this area means the message that Black & Grey will convey to their target market will be weak.

They are again not alone! This is a breakdown of what will be included (or not included) as part of their overall message...

1. Unique Perceived Benefit

They agree that fixed price quotes are their uniqueness.

At least they've tried to hang their hat on something.

46

But although many businesses do not adopt this approach (even though they should), this is not uniqueness. Unfortunately Black & Grey believe it is enough to do the job of a UPB. It isn't!

They also believe that saying things like 'proactive', 'personal service', 'value', 'reliability', 'support' and 'service second to none' will strike a chord with potential customers. Again they're wrong – very wrong. We call the use of these vague statements 'puffery'. Any business can say these things (and most do) so none of this sets the business apart from the competition. And, more importantly, none of it makes the potential customer sit up and think – wow!

Furthermore, they believe they should always list the types of widgets they provide. Again this is a common practice adopted by most businesses. For example, here's an extensive list of commonly used terms an accountant may list (and in no particular order)...

- Business Planning
- Raising Finance
- Profit Improvement
- Bookkeeping & Payroll
- Audit & Accounting Services
- Tax Planning
- Start-Ups
- Self-Employed
- Partnerships
- Limited Liability Company
- Corporations
- Support Services
- Personal Tax Preparation

You have to think about this logically. It's like seeing an ad for a butcher saying 'we do all kinds of meat'. You're just stating the obvious – and none of it is compelling.

Customers and potential customers expect all these things as standard. The only time you should mention a particular product or service is if it is genuinely unique and one that will help you generate interest. Otherwise you are wasting your time. A list of products or services DOES NOT WORK in attracting people to your business and DOES NOT POSITION YOU DIFFERENTLY FROM EVERY OTHER BUSINESS!

2. Features Into Benefits

It's always interesting to look in the Yellow Pages and review what each business lists as benefits. Do it yourself now. Turn to your category (or any other for that matter) and look at each ad. What benefits are listed? Do you see any?

For example, a list of 'services' is NOT a list of benefits. The fact that you work with different types of businesses is not a benefit. A 'Free no-obligation meeting' is not a benefit. 'Fixed Price Quotes' is not a benefit.

Now since Black & Grey are constructing their uniqueness around 'Fixed Price Quotes' (they genuinely believe this is a UPB) – they are currently simply stating the feature.

The benefit for this feature would be something like...

"You know to the penny how much you will pay for our widgets. There are never any nasty shocks. You can budget accordingly and relax in the knowledge that our quotes are fixed."

Look at the difference between this and just saying 'fixed price quotes'. You've transformed a dull, one-dimensional feature into a more exciting emotional appeal.

3. Irresistible Offer

We can't get around the fact that you want to meet with potential customers. As we said earlier, a 'Free No-Obligation Meeting' in itself isn't a benefit, but it is an offer.

Black & Grey are going to persist in offering this as their key offer.

But remember, virtually EVERY business that meets with potential customers offers this. It's like personal injury lawyers making a big deal out of 'no win, no fee'. Because everyone offers this you have to change it, add something to it, or add some kind of value to it. Otherwise the potential customer will not be moved to do anything.

4. Headline

Since Black & Grey doesn't understand the importance of having a compelling headline as part of the message, they do what 80% of businesses do, and simply use the name of their business.

If you don't believe us, look back at your Yellow Pages and count how many ads have weak, meaningless or clever headlines, or the name of the business as the headline.

No matter how long your business has been operating, and no matter how successful it is – the name of your business will never grab the attention of a prospective customer as much as a powerful headline. Leading with the business's name is a sure way to reduce your marketing to zero effectiveness. You've been warned!

5. Guarantee

Black & Grey does not know the value of guarantees or why they should even use them. They offer good levels of service – so why bother?

The point is, however, that guarantees, in the mind of the prospective customer, demonstrate that you stand behind everything you do. Remember, until they start using you, a customer won't know how good you or your products or services are.

If you can reassure the prospective customer that you have a strong guarantee which demonstrates to them that you DO deliver on your promises, then this is one more reason why they should choose you over and above any other business.

6. Sales Barrier Demolition

Black & Grey isn't even aware of this (nor would they be – it's something we have created, that's unique to us).

7. Reasons Why

Since Black & Grey doesn't have any real irresistible offers or startling guarantees then, even though they aren't aware of the importance of reasons why, their message will be devoid of any.

8. Social Proof

The good news is that Black & Grey do use testimonials (two). They do understand their importance and they will be part of their message. Unfortunately they've committed a common mistake and presented their testimonials in a way which achieves the opposite of what they should do (build credibility). For example, here's how they present each testimonial...

> "I have used Black & Grey for over five years for our business. Their professionalism has been exemplary. They adopt a 'can-do' attitude and are prepared to go the extra mile to satisfy a customer. Having used larger national suppliers in the past, the level of service I receive from Black & Grey is most gratifying and I know the answer to any question I have is only a telephone call away. I have no hesitation in recommending them to

```
anyone. Nice people to do business with
and they make life much less taxing!"

AS - Stourbridge
```

Can you see what's wrong with this?

The testimonial itself is actually quite good. It builds credibility and highlights a number of valuable attributes.

Unfortunately Black & Grey, for some reason, have reduced the full name to just initials and omitted the company name.

This is very common. And it's a big mistake.

This renders the testimonial meaningless and in fact can do the business more harm than good. By choosing to omit the actual source of the testimonial, the potential customer doesn't believe it, or at least doubts its authenticity.

Black & Grey are a member of a well-known widget association so will use this to add credibility, which is a wise decision.

9. Call To Action

Black & Grey doesn't realize how important the Call To Action is, so their marketing pieces and their message won't include a powerful one. Instead they will just mention the phone number and possibly their web address.

Rainbow Widgets

"So once you've settled on your target market the message you convey to them is all-important. Most people don't realize that for a message to compel a prospective customer to respond to you, it needs these nine Marketing Assets.

"But it's not just about including them in your message. It's also about making sure they are included correctly. How you do it is as important as what you do.

"So let's take a look at how to ensure the Marketing Assets combine to give you a compelling message.

"Now at the moment you suffer from the same affliction as most other businesses, in that you don't have a uniqueness. You don't differentiate your business from the competition.

"This, although right now you may not think so, has serious consequences. You see, not being seen as being different not only makes it harder for you to acquire customers – it makes their decision-making harder too and leads them to one horrible but common conclusion on the only way they can choose you over and above other businesses.

"So to make you understand this further, let's just go through the following scenario.

"Let's turn the tables and say you're running a business and you're looking for a new supplier of the widgets you sell. So you ask your friends if they can recommend a good one, but none of them can. So where would you go to find a supplier?

"That's right, most likely the internet or the Yellow Pages. But let's say you choose the internet.

"You type into Google 'widget in <your town>' and dozens of businesses are listed. You then systematically start clicking on each business to have a look at them to see which one jumps out at you. But it's not easy for you to choose who to contact. Is it?

"Why?

"That's right, because all the websites say the same things. None of the businesses differentiate. None of the businesses target your type of business as a key target market. Everyone is just listing their widgets. No one is saying choose us, we're different because...!

"Now you have a dilemma. How do you choose the three businesses you're going to call to hopefully meet with?

"It's not easy, but you use what seems to be a logical process. You choose three businesses that are closest to you and seem to 'look' like they are professional and can deal with you and your business. You don't know you're doing this, but you also look for clues on who would be the best business to work with. These clues are the Marketing Assets, such as headlines, testimonials, guarantees and the like. But while the three businesses you've chosen seem to be the best, none of them actually provide compelling reasons for you to get in touch. But this doesn't perturb you. You've managed to whittle your list down to three businesses. Now you're ready to call them.

"You call each business with a view to making an appointment. In fairness all three companies handle the call equally well and you make an appointment to meet with all three.

"Then you meet with each one, and although all of them seem to know what they're talking about, no one really tells you why you should use them. Why they're different. Why they're better for you than any other business.
"Does this sound familiar?

"They all say they'll write to you confirming what their prices are. They'll send you a quote.

"You now eagerly await the quotes. And as promised, they all arrive a couple of days after the meeting. Yet again the quotes all look the same, with one difference – the price is different on each quote. (See below.)

A Typical Quotation – How <u>NOT</u> To Do It

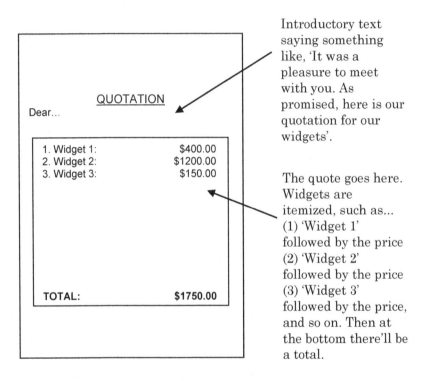

Introductory text saying something like, 'It was a pleasure to meet with you. As promised, here is our quotation for our widgets'.

The quote goes here. Widgets are itemized, such as... (1) 'Widget 1' followed by the price (2) 'Widget 2' followed by the price (3) 'Widget 3' followed by the price, and so on. Then at the bottom there'll be a total.

"Remember, none of these businesses have taken the time or made the effort to differentiate themselves. And that's the dilemma faced by you – the prospective customer. You see, because you believe all the businesses are the SAME you now have just one justifiable and real way to differentiate between all three businesses.

"Any idea?

"Yes, that's right – PRICE.

"Because none of the businesses have differentiated themselves, the only way the prospect can make a decision is based on price. That doesn't necessarily mean they choose the lowest price (more on this later), but it creates an artificial situation where the owners of the businesses (and the industry at large) believe that price is becoming THE significant factor when choosing a supplier. Price of course plays a part in all purchasing decisions (more so for a small percentage of people who always buy the cheapest) but when you don't differentiate, you force the prospective customer down the price route – which ISN'T THEIR FAULT. And of course it gets worse when the economy struggles.

"It's YOUR fault. So now when you think your market seems to be price-sensitive or you feel under pressure with prices, you understand why, and in many cases this can be avoided simply by differentiating your business from every other business.

"This becomes more powerful when your differentiation is focused on your identified target market(s) and you are giving them something they genuinely desire. This is the secret to differentiation: give the target market something they highly desire that no other business can offer. Do that and you have the makings of a message that will be magnetic to your target market.

"We've given you the 10 methods for creating your uniqueness. What you need to think about now is what could you focus on that will be highly attractive to your target market and at the same time be difficult for your competition to copy or exploit.

"That takes us nicely on to benefits. These are the things that add 'sizzle to the steak'. Your benefits should leap out at the target market and reinforce to them that you are the business to go to. Of course the more relevant and meaningful the benefits are to your target market – the more importance they will have.

"So you've now got a UPB and a set of benefits that are focused on your target market. Are you starting to see why choosing the right target market(s) in the first place is so important? What you're doing is creating a message that is so laser-focused on the target market, that when your message is delivered to them, you're making it very hard for the recipient to say 'no'. This is target marketing at its best.

"Next is your offer. Now as we said earlier we can't get away from the fact that ultimately you're going to be offering a free no-obligation meeting. But there's so much you can do to make your offer much more appealing than any other business.

"The first question to ask yourself when trying to craft an irresistible offer is this: 'What can I offer that positions me as an expert and at the same time is desirable for my target market?'

"You have to forget about the meeting for a second to be able to do this. Let us put it another way... what can you give your target market that makes them think 'wow, this business is a real expert in my field'?

"By far and away the best thing you can do that adds enormous credibility, and positions you as an expert with your target market, is to create a publication. This can take the form of a number of things, from a printed book to special reports and articles. A book of course gives you the ultimate credibility but articles, and special reports in particular, can achieve similar results. For example, let's say your target market is based on businesses with a revenue of $250k to $500k. Your special report could be entitled 'Little-Known Secrets That Businesses Under $500k Should Be Aware Of Before Choosing A Widget Supplier'. Now, to a business owner who is turning over, say, under $500k, this report is irresistible. You now have the makings of something very powerful to give as part of your overall offer.

"Your report can have any title as long as it clearly identifies the target market you're seeking. You'll offer your report as part of the incentive for a potential customer to meet with you. You're already starting to move away from the competition when it comes to the offer. Here's how you take it to the next level.

"Since everyone else is offering a 'free meeting', you need to do something different that again makes meeting with you more favorable than meeting with anyone else. You do this by explaining in simple terms WHY giving up 90 minutes of their time will be so valuable to them. Tell them that during the meeting you'll be able to give them 2 or 3 pearls of wisdom about their business that they never knew and they can take away with them. Tell them that because you work with their type of businesses day in, day out, you know how they tick and you can give them tips that will improve how they use and benefit from your widgets. You do this automatically anyway (you're good at what you do), but telling them this up-front makes a huge difference to their decision-making process.

"The final piece of the jigsaw really sets you apart. Tell them that if they don't think this is the most worthwhile meeting they've had in the last 12 months, you'll write a check for $200 made out to their favorite charity. Now you're guaranteeing the meeting will be of immense value and indirectly you're putting a cost on their time.

"We then complete the offer equation by clearly stating that your free special report, worth $97, is only available for free during the next 21 days. This is your 'stimulator'. You use this to reduce procrastination.

"So now you have an irresistible offer. You've got a report which adds credibility and positions you as an expert. You have several reasons why the meeting will be so worthwhile. You have a guarantee and you have a stimulator. Compare that to the norm. Compare that to Black & Grey who like every other business are simply offering a 'no-obligation meeting'. Who would you rather meet, and we're only a third of the way towards completing your message? This is very powerful stuff.

"Next, the headlines you use need to grab attention. We've explained that the headline is one of the most important elements of the message because it forces the recipient to read/listen to or watch what you have to say. A poor headline means no matter how good your message, the target market will simply pass you by. Think of it like you're waiting for a bus to stop. You can wait by a proper bus stop (the headline) and 99 times out of 100 the bus will stop and let you on. Or you can take your chances and stand anywhere in the street, hold your hand out and hope the bus will stop. You might get lucky 5 times in every 100. That's the difference between a good and a bad headline.

"And like everything else, your headline needs to connect with the target market. So, if your target market is 'start-ups', then a headline such as 'Attention Start-Ups: How You Too Can Create A Thriving Business' will attract more attention with the target market than a more general headline 'How You Too Can Create A Thriving Business'. Compare these two to the headline 'Black & Grey'.

"When you see it like this, hopefully you can immediately understand why the headline plays such an important role, and why the name of your business really is the worst headline you could ever use!

"If prospects or customers dismiss the headline – that's it, you've lost them. They won't start reading your letter, ad, brochure, etc., or listening to your telephone script or radio ad – and you won't get a response or a sale.

"To emphasize the importance of headlines, here are a couple of quotes from two of the most highly respected copywriters of all time...

> **"If you can come up with a good headline, you are almost sure to have a good ad. But even the greatest writer can't save an ad with a poor headline."**
>
> John Caples - How To Make Your Advertising Make Money
>
> **"On average five times as many people read the headline as read the body copy."**
>
> David Ogilvy - Confessions Of An Advertising Man

"What does this mean? Basically, if you get your headline right you almost guarantee your success. Get your headline wrong - and your results will suffer!

"Here's a simple example to show how few people understand the basic principle of using headlines...

"We've just picked up a copy of the Yellow Pages directory. We're looking in the Accounting category. These are the 'headlines' of the ads on one page:

- Pearson Jones

- Powlett & Smith

- R Graham & Co

- Richard Prentice Partnership

- Sturgeon Simpson & Co

- Shappleton Accountants

- Shardrake Fellows

– S.R. Connaught

– Running your own business

"With the exception of the last headline, the headline for each ad is the name of the business that's advertising.

"Because so many people are doing it wrong, if all you do is lead with a strong headline on all your marketing communications, you'll improve the response and success many times over.

Effective Headlines Fulfill These Four Key Objectives...

- Get attention
- Select an audience
- Deliver a complete message
- Draw the reader into the body copy (or keep them listening to you, etc.)

"The good news is that creating winning headlines can be achieved by following some simple and proven 'headline types'. We've listed seven of the most successful ones here. By applying a number of these different headline types you'll start to see how you can create winning headlines...

- **Benefit headlines** (all your headlines should contain a benefit of some sort)

- **Use a two- or three-word headline** (but remember long headlines are almost always more successful then short headlines)

    – Get One Month Free
      Double Bonus Service
    – Oh My God!
    – Gosh
    – At Last

     – Millionaire Secrets
     – If Only…

- **Headlines that focus on quick and easy solutions**

     – Fast And Simple…
     – Ridiculously Easy And Fast…
     – Idiot-Proof…
     – In Just 10 Days…
     – The 7-Minute Workout…
     – The Lazy Man's Way To…
     – Instant, Automatic Results…
     – The Quick And Easy Way To…

- **Warning headlines**

     – Read This Before You…
     – Don't Choose Another Accountant Until You've Read These Facts

- **Testimonial headlines**

     – A Specific Benefit Written Testimonial From One Of Your Customers
     – "Or It Can Just Be A Headline In Quotation Marks Like This Written Like A Testimonial"

- **Reasons why headlines**

     – Seven Reasons Why You Should…
     – 37 Invigorating Reasons…
     – 6 Ways To…
     – 7 Steps…
     – Here's How…

- **Offer headlines**

> – Put your offer in the headline...
> – Try-Before-You-Buy Accounting Service

"Now let's talk about guarantees.

"As you know, the benefit of your product or service is gained **after** the sale is made. After you've acquired the customer. Sometimes this can be days, weeks, months or even years after the first sale was made (depending on what you sell). This in itself places a risk on the shoulders of would-be customers. It's this risk that often prevents them from buying or moving from one business to the next – even though they're not happy.

"However, if you lower or eliminate this risk, then the natural consequence is people will be more inclined to buy from you.

"That's the secret of creating a powerful guarantee that reverses the risk.

"A guarantee is nothing more than simply taking away the barriers from the sale and ensures that the prospect keeps progressing towards the sale.

"As soon as you add a guarantee it removes the risks of buying, ensuring more customers are gained. It automatically differentiates the business from the competition. And it adds value.

"Prospects will value your services much more because they'll assume the service must live up to expectations, and the business must be excellent at delivering the service ('Why would they offer a guarantee if the product or service wasn't great?').

"The result is therefore a BIG increase in new customers!

5. How Do We Get People Interested?

"The ultimate aim is to guarantee the result or main benefit of your service and add a 'penalty' should the service fail to live up to your promises.

"Here's how it looks...

Perfect Guarantee =	Guarantee the result or benefit of your service	+	Penalize your business if result not achieved

"Just to explain this further, here's a simple example of how risk reversal works. A man wants to buy a puppy for his daughter. He responds to two ads in the local newspaper. He examines the first puppy and it seems ideal in temperament and looks. The owner says to the man, 'If the dog isn't right for your daughter, bring it back in one week and I'll give you your money back.' Clearly he appreciated the value of risk reversal but he didn't fully understand it!

"The man then goes to look at the second puppy. Again it seems ideal in temperament and looks. Only this time the owner says, 'Your daughter is obviously looking forward to her new puppy and it's important that she's totally happy with it. Please take the puppy, let your daughter play with it, look after it, and get to know it. If after three weeks the puppy is not right for her, bring the puppy back, and I'll refund your money in full and give you $25 for your time, effort and trouble.'

"Now this man really understands risk reversal. First he extended the 'trial' period. He knows that his puppy is a good dog. He also knows after three weeks the puppy and girl will be inseparable. He totally reverses the risk.

"You also need to understand this. The company that reverses the risk, automatically gains competitive advantage and wins more business – in fact much more! This competitive advantage is very significant when attracting new customers to your business.

"Here's another example, it's one of the best we've ever seen. It's from a pest control company called BBBK. Their guarantee is aimed at hotels and restaurants but again you can adopt something similar for your own business.

> You don't owe one penny until all the pests on your premises have been eradicated...if you are ever dissatisfied with BBBK's services you will receive a refund for up to 12 months of the company's services...plus fees for another exterminator of your choice for the next year.
>
> If a guest spots a pest on your premises, BBBK will pay for the guest's meal or room, send a letter of apology, and pay for a future meal or stay...and if your facility is closed down due to the presence of roaches or
>
> rodents, BBBK will pay any fines, as well as all lost profits, plus $5,000.

"Although we don't know for certain, it's easy to **assume** several things about BBBK from this guarantee. They are very good at pest control. They understand the concerns of their customers with regard to hygiene. They are very successful at attracting new customers! They are probably providing very similar services to their competitors. However, they understand risk reversal. Their **profits,** we're sure, will reflect this!

"Let's put this into your terms...

> "We guarantee to deliver all our widgets to you on time, every time. We agree with you, in advance, a date for delivery and if we fail to meet that date, you don't pay a single penny. They're absolutely free! What's more, if at any time you are dissatisfied with the quality of the widgets, simply send them

> back for a full refund or instant replacement. No
> arguments, no objection."

"Hopefully you now have a basic grasp of guarantees and what they can achieve for your business. If you've given any thought to the strategy, several questions may be entering your mind.

"For example, 'Won't people try to abuse what I am offering?' and 'Won't I lose a lot of money with this?' The key, of course, to successful guarantees is this – if you offer a good product or service (which you do) then you have nothing to worry about.

"Unfortunately we cannot say no one will ask for a refund or for their money back (or whatever your guarantee states). What we can say is that, for every one of these, you will attract many more prospects and customers by simply offering a guarantee in the first place.

"Your guarantee is usually the one thing that tips the scales in your favor. Because you offer a guarantee, your prospect thinks and assumes the following things about you. First, if you're offering this guarantee, you must be very good at what you do. And second, you would be 'foolish' to offer such a guarantee if you were poor at delivering your promises.

"In the prospect's mind the guarantee has 'proven' to him or her that you can give them exactly what they need. More importantly, when most people choose to buy any product or service, they choose it for perfectly good reasons and intentions. And they spend time making their decision. They wouldn't choose you in the first place if they wanted to capitalize on the guarantee.

"Therefore you should be thinking about guaranteeing the products or services you provide. Guaranteeing delivery times on work.   Guaranteeing support services. You name it, whatever you do and how you do it – you can guarantee it, and the bolder you are – the better.

"That takes us nicely onto Sales Barrier Demolition. One guarantee on its own can do wonders for you, but a multi-layered guarantee – or as we prefer to call it, a Sales Barrier Demolition Guarantee – has the ability to take your business to unprecedented heights. Probably the best way to demonstrate this to you is by taking an example from another industry and show you how powerful a multi-layered guarantee can become.

"This is the Sales Barrier Demolition for a kitchen replacement company. They don't completely strip out the kitchen. They simple replace the doors, drawers, worktops, sinks, etc., and by doing so give the kitchen a whole new facelift for a fraction of the cost of a brand new kitchen.

"A successful Sales Barrier Demolition Strategy focuses on the pressing fears, worries and frustrations that customers have in terms of the industry at large. So for example, a kitchen replacement company is a contractor, and people have fears such as: they don't start when they say they're going to start; they will leave the job unfinished; they will pay more than they were quoted; they'll leave a mess every day; they won't finish on time, and so on.

"So by focusing on these fears we can create a compelling Sales Barrier Demolition like this.

Our Unrivalled 7-Point Guarantee...

1. We guarantee we'll start when we say we will

2. We guarantee we'll start every morning when we say we will

3. We guarantee we'll leave your kitchen tidy and clean at the end of each day

4.   We guarantee we'll never leave your kitchen until we've finished it

5.   We guarantee we'll finish your kitchen when we say we will

6.   We guarantee your bill will be as quoted – not a penny more

7.   We guarantee our products and workmanship for five years

"Now read that again. If you were looking for a kitchen replacement company, don't you think this would be extremely attractive to you? Note, price doesn't come into it!

"Then, to give it extra oomph, you completely reverse the risk so the customer doesn't take any risk should the business NOT deliver on its promises. Instead you're putting the risk on your shoulders (reversing the risk).

"Here's how it's done (the words in bold show you the added elements).

*Our Unrivalled 7-Point **MONEY-BACK** Guarantee...*

1.   We guarantee we'll start when we say we will

2.   We guarantee we'll start every morning when we say we will

3.   We guarantee we'll leave your kitchen tidy and clean at the end of each day

4.   We guarantee we'll never leave your kitchen until we've finished it

5.   We guarantee we'll finish your kitchen when we say we will

6.   We guarantee your bill will be as quoted – not a penny more

7.   We guarantee our products and workmanship for five years

If we don't deliver on all 7 guarantees 100% of the time – you don't pay us a single penny. In other words, your kitchen is FREE if we 'foul up'.

"When you use a sensational guarantee, offer or sales barrier demolition it is important to back it up with what we call 'Reasons Why'. We require 'reasons why' because, unless you tell people why you offer such things, they can dismiss what you're saying, they think it's too good to be true. So your 'reasons why' validates and makes your message sound believable.

"For example, here's the 'reasons why' that you could have for the sales barrier demolition above.

So why would we do this? Simple. The guarantee states in the open our high level of service. Last year we refurbished 2,314 kitchens. Not one of our customers got their kitchen for free.

That means one thing – we deliver on our promises, and I'm sure you'll agree in our industry this is rare. So for us our guarantee isn't a risk; but for you it delivers complete peace of mind. And that's important – very important.

"Do you see what we're doing here? The 'Reasons Why' actually supports and validates the Sales Barrier Demolition strategy, but, equally as important, it's a very powerful sales tool and marketing asset!

"What further supports your message and proves that you do deliver on your promises is the use of Social Proof. Customer testimonials and other credibility builders are key ingredients that add believability.

"We note that you have a couple of testimonials – but once you've identified your target market, you need to get testimonials from other customers that fit the target market.

"Once again it's this tailoring of your message to fit the target market that will help you get big leaps in customer acquisitions of the right type of customers. For example, if your target market is businesses with revenue of $250k to $500k, the only testimonials you should be using are from businesses of a similar size. We cannot overstate the importance of this. Relevance is a key motivator, so the more relevant everything is to the target market – the more appealing you'll become.

"Furthermore, your testimonials should ideally stress a number of your key benefits. The more positive the reinforcement of your overall offer – the better.

"Now you may think getting customer testimonials is challenging. It's not. Simply write to the relevant customers and ask them to give you a few comments about what they like about your business, and ask for their permission to use their comments on your material. You'll be surprised at the responses you get, and how good the comments are.

"Then once you've got your supply of testimonials, simply use the ones which convey your benefits best. It really is that simple!

"And finally we complete our message by using a powerful 'Call To Action'. The purpose of every marketing piece is simple: you must get the recipient to act and you must get them to act now!

"Getting anyone to DO something isn't easy. In fact, responding is usually inconvenient. More often than not the prospect or customer is busy. Other things are more important.

"It's very easy for your prospect to say to themselves, 'I'll reply tomorrow.' But as we all know, tomorrow never comes!

"Therefore your number one goal is to get a response now. Your call to action is all-important in achieving this objective. Tests have proved that without a call to action your marketing piece is likely to be 50% less effective – that's how important the Call To Action is.

"As we mentioned earlier, a good Call To Action summarizes the offer, explains what the recipient needs to do to act now and includes the stimulator to reduce procrastination.

"Working hard at creating a powerful message by including all the marketing assets will be time very well spent. We guarantee as long as you include each of the marketing assets on every one of your marketing pieces – you'll see a significant increase in results."

Key Summary & Action Points

1. Once you've identified the target market(s), your message should be tailored to focus completely on it.

2. A powerful message is created by using all 9 of the Marketing Assets: (1) UPB, (2) Benefits, (3) Irresistible Offer, (4) Headline, (5) Guarantee, (6) Sales Barrier Demolition, (7) Reasons Why, (8) Social Proof, (9) Call To Action.

3. Time and effort spent on creating well-constructed Marketing Assets will result in a significant improvement in your results.

6. What Marketing Pieces Should We Use To Deliver Our Message?

Introduction

Over the years we've noticed that very few people give any great thought to the types of media they should be using to deliver their message to the target market. More often than not, they simply use the same media that all their competitors are using.

This could mean two things...

- In most cases the <u>best</u> media isn't being used, and as a result, neither are the best marketing pieces being used to the right target market(s).

- Existing marketing pieces are wasteful.

Furthermore, there can be a huge difference in results if you don't choose the correct media. It's been our experience that many companies leave small fortunes on the table, simply because they have failed to choose the correct media.

The good news is that once you've defined the media (we call this a 'Media Channel') the marketing pieces select themselves (Method – see next agenda item)!

This is a very simple yet highly effective way to determine the right Media Channels to use for your business.

First let's look at the Media Channels available to you. As you can see, there are just three main Media Channel Categories...

Media Channel Category	Media Channel
1. Published Media	• Classifieds • Newspaper, Magazine & Business Press • Yellow Pages® • Inserts • Radio • TV • Press Releases • Etc.
2. Direct Marketing Media	• Fax • Seminars • Sales Letters • Lead Generation Letters • Postcards • Flyers • Joint Ventures • Newsletters • Leaflets • Telemarketing • Networking • Etc.
3. E-Media	• Website • Search Engines • Pay Per Click Search Engines • Social Media • eBay • Etc.

So how do you choose the right Media Channel Category and combination of Media Channels for your business?

6. What marketing Pieces Should We Use?

All you need to do is ask yourself the following two simple questions...

"Where can the target market be reached?"

"Where would the target market look to source our products/services?"

The answers to these two questions will help you to determine which Media Channel and marketing pieces to use...

CHOOSING THE RIGHT MEDIA CHANNELS		
Where can the target market be found?	**Media Category**	**Media Channel**
At work (or in the business)	Direct Marketing Media	• Fax • Seminars • Sales Letter • Postcards • Flyers • Joint Ventures • Newsletters • Leaflets • Telemarketing
At home	Direct Marketing Media	• Fax (you wouldn't use fax because very few people have fax machines at home unless the target market was 'people with offices at home')

		• Seminars • Sales Letter • Postcards • Flyers • Joint Ventures • Newsletters • Leaflets • Telemarketing
Yellow Pages	Published Media	• Yellow Pages®
Business Press	Published Media	• Classifieds • Business Press • Inserts • Press Releases
Internet	E-Media	• Website • Search Engines • Pay Per Click Search Engines • Social Media
Local newspaper	Published Media	• Classifieds • Newspaper • Inserts • Press Releases

And as you can see from the table above, once you've created your Media Channel list you can then very easily select your marketing pieces for each media.

Black & Grey Widgets

Black & Grey doesn't really understand the true implications of choosing the correct media and the positive effect using multiple media can have on the growth of the business.

So they decide to use 'direct marketing media' and 'e-media' but don't give any thought to how best they can reach their target market.

Rainbow Widgets

"You see, once you ask and answer these two questions, you can choose the right media to reach your target market. It really is that simple, but this is one of the most important steps you can take.

"Of course, because people prefer to consume different media and prefer to respond to different media, you never know which is best for each individual, which is why we advocate a multi-media approach. Again tests have shown that mixing media, as opposed to using just one, significantly increases results.

"Therefore you will use all 3 media categories to deliver your message to the target market."

Key Summary & Action Points

1. There are three media categories (1) Published Media, (2) Direct Marketing Media and (3) E-Media.

2. Because people differ in what media they consume, you should use all three media categories to deliver your message to the target market.

Why Businesses Stop Growing...

7. How Many Times Should We Contact The Target Market?

Introduction

There has been much debate about how many times prospects should be contacted. There is no definitive answer, but what we do know is it needs to be more than once – several more. To explain why you need multiple contacts, you need to first understand a little-known but proven phenomenon (we call it the 'Moment') that when used correctly will multiply the number of inquiries and ultimately new customers you get.

It also goes some way to explaining why most people think marketing doesn't work. 'Moment' is the fourth of the '5 Ms Of Marketing Your Business'.

So let's start with a simple question...

How many times a year do you currently contact your target market?

If it's any number less than 12 you're turning away thousands and thousands of dollars in sales and profits.

It is highly unlikely that you will have sent a marketing piece to any of your potential customers EVERY month – indeed our research has shown that businesses who do bother to market to their potential customers, on average only send 1 or 2 pieces a year to them.

THIS IS ANOTHER REASON WHY MOST MARKETING DOESN'T WORK.

Why Businesses Stop Growing...

Tests have proved that repetitive marketing yields far greater returns than ad-hoc marketing. That's why our recommendation is for you to send a marketing piece every month to your potential customers. This will give you the best results.

Why does this work so well?

Repetitive marketing takes advantage of what we call the 'The Moving Parade'. It exists in every market and industry, but fewer than 1 in 10,000 businesses are aware of it, or how to use it in order to quickly grow their businesses.

So what is 'The Moving Parade' and how can you use it to your advantage?

Selling any product or service is all about timing. Just because someone isn't interested in buying the product or service today, it doesn't mean they aren't going to be interested tomorrow.

That is in essence what 'The Moving Parade' is all about. Let us explain this further...

Let's say that at the moment you're really happy with your car. You've got no intention of changing it. Therefore every advertisement, every mailing or any contact you have with a car dealer or car manufacturer is wasted on you.

Letters go in the trash without a second thought. You pick up your newspaper when the advertisements come on TV. You simply aren't interested. And nothing will prompt you at this stage to even consider changing your car.

However, three months later your circumstances have changed. You need to do more travelling, and so you decide it's time to look for a more suitable car.

Now every mailing, advertisement, or communication to do with cars is instantly given attention by you. You're 'in the market' for a new car and you develop an insatiable appetite to find out as much as you can about the cars which would suit you best.

This happens all day, every day, as people buy products and services.

If you don't keep in touch regularly with your prospects (and customers) you'll never get 'lucky' with the timing as people move in and out of the market, depending on changing circumstances (see diagram on the next page).

By keeping in contact at least once every month the chance that you will hit the prospect at the right time is increased tenfold.

The fear that many people have is that they will be seen to be somehow 'unprofessional' by bombarding their target market with junk mail. Well, we have news for you...

Marketing your business effectively is about as professional as you can get. Thoughtful use of our Marketing Assets will only improve the market's perception of your business, so providing you don't breach ethical guidelines (and nothing we advocate does this) then you can only win – and win BIG!

Taking advantage of The Moving Parade is a very-easy-to-use strategy and one that will provide excellent results for businesses who grasp it. So, as we mentioned earlier, our recommendation is for you to send one stand-out marketing piece every month to your target market. This will automatically result in big increases in inquiries and sales for your business.

The Moving Parade – What It Looks Like

People/Businesses Who Aren't In A Position To Buy – AT THE MOMENT
These people outside the 'Buying Mode' circle are in your target market or niche but for a number of reasons they will not buy at the moment.

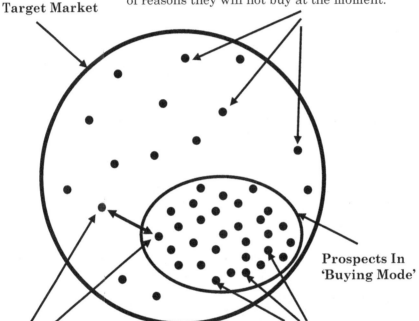

Target Market

Prospects In 'Buying Mode'

The Moving Parade: People/Businesses That Either Become Buyers Or Non-Buyers
People or businesses move in and out of 'buying mode' all the time. Circumstances change, resulting in people or businesses either becoming buyers or non-buyers. This movement in and out of 'buying mode' is what we call

People/Businesses Who Are Ready To Buy Right Now
These people inside the 'Buying Mode' circle are ready to buy right now – remember, they can only buy from YOU or your competitors.

Using a range of stand-out marketing pieces helps you win a large proportion of

7. How Many Times Should We Make Contact?

The Result
Using The Moving Parade to your advantage by constantly keeping in touch with the target market, and your customers, means when movement occurs out of non-buying mode into buying mode by any prospect, you have a high probability of getting the sale.

Black & Grey Widgets

Unfortunately Black & Grey have no idea about The Moving Parade and like most other businesses hope that one or at the most two approaches to their target market will suffice. They may get lucky but the level of response they receive will be low – very low.

Rainbow Widgets

"This is one of the most important things you can learn when growing your business. The Moving Parade is such an important phenomenon that you have to use it to your advantage.

"The only way to do that is to set up a frequency of contact that takes away the 'luck' factor and instead enables you to have a contact strategy that maximizes the chances of you 'catching' someone, just when they're thinking of either changing their current supplier or buying for the first time.

"Remember, you have no way of knowing when a prospect's circumstances are about to change. It could be an unexpected invoice or a missed deadline. It could be an unsatisfactory resolution to a problem or just a mistake. Or just a culmination of a small number of things that cause frustration. But no matter what the circumstance, you have to give yourself the best chance of getting the inquiry. The only way to do that is to get your business's name in front of them at regular intervals throughout the year. That's the only way we know how to get 'lucky'. But boy does it work!

"With one marketing piece you may only get 0.5% or less as a response. But with 12 or more well-constructed marketing pieces, strategically sent to the prospect throughout the year, responses will often multiply.

"We recommend a minimum of 12 contacts sent to your target market – one every month."

Key Summary & Action Points

1. The Moving Parade is an important phenomenon that explains how a change in circumstances leads to people moving in and out of 'buying mode'.

2. You can take advantage of The Moving Parade by contacting your target market several times a year (ideally 12 or more times per year).

---

8. How Do We Create Marketing Pieces That Get Results?

Introduction

We have now reached the last of the '5 Ms Of Marketing Your Business'.

This last 'M' is another big reason why so many marketing campaigns fail – the method used in the media to deliver the message just doesn't work.

In other words, you could have got all previous 'M's in place - right market, right message, right media and right moment - but the actual device itself just doesn't work.

For example, all 4 'M's are in place, yet let's say the advertisement used in the magazine wasn't put together using all the Marketing Assets, and those that were included weren't used correctly. You see, not only do all the Marketing Assets need to be used in each marketing piece – there is also a RIGHT and WRONG way to create the piece itself.

This final piece of the jigsaw is so, so important. It also includes how you get your marketing piece noticed. For example, numerous tests have shown that using handwritten names and addresses and multiple stamps on the front of an envelope works more than 9 times better (that's NOT a mistake!) than a label and a postage machine.

So to get results from your marketing pieces they have to be created, based on the following three elements (otherwise they will fail – or at least won't work as well as you'd hoped)...

- <u>Marketing Assets</u> – all the marketing assets must be included as your message.

- <u>The Right Format</u> – we spoke earlier about the right and wrong ways of creating each marketing piece.

- <u>Stand-Out Appeal</u> – if your marketing piece doesn't rise above the clutter and get noticed it will die a horrible death (most marketing pieces never pass this test).

Black & Grey Widgets

Like most people and most businesses, Black & Grey take the view that they will be able to create their own marketing pieces. There's nothing wrong with this at all, but if you do go down the 'do it yourself' route you must invest some time and money in relevant books, seminars and courses to see how to do it.

For the cost of just $20 or $30 you can buy a book written by an expert that shows you how to create ads, sales letters, seminars, websites, you name it – and as long as you research wisely, for less than a good meal for two you can give yourself a much better chance of success.

Yet most people won't even do this. Sure there are many books full of worthless theories on how to do it, but books like this one, where the author(s) has genuinely been there, done it and got the T-shirt and will give you the 'tricks of the trade', DO exist!

But Black & Grey do what most people do and decide to create their marketing pieces 'in-house'. After all, they think, it can't be that hard to get results. But without seeking out expertise even in the form of a book, their chances of success are low – very low.

Rainbow Widgets

"As we mentioned above, it's the combination of these three elements which helps to transform any marketing piece into a winner. And often it takes trial and error to achieve success. We've explained about the 9 Marketing Assets and what you need to do to create them.

"Next, the right format is crucial for your marketing pieces to be successful. For example, almost every website fails in terms of generating inquiries. In all our years not one business owner has come to us and said, 'I have a great website that keeps churning out inquiries'. That's because the format is wrong. All wrong.

"You see, aesthetically and functionality wise, most websites are fine. The problem occurs because they are created not to generate inquiries but to look impressive and show a professional image of the business. Sure a site like this adds credibility (an important element) but without a focus on generating inquiries, it fails to deliver.

"So what do you do to make it work? This is the 'how' and it's not that difficult. All you need is a stand-alone web page that focuses on your target market and then delivers the message to them using the Marketing Assets. The single goal of that page could be for people to download your free report, etc. (remember your irresistible offer?) or to generate the inquiry or the sale. Tests have repeatedly shown that there should be no outgoing links to any other page or website. Complete focus on the objective is what brings results.

"But to really make your marketing pieces work they have to stand out. This is the third and final piece of the success jigsaw. You see, not only does your business have to differentiate itself from the competition to attract and retain customers – the same can be said about your marketing.

"People are subjected to hundreds of marketing messages every day. You have to rise above this 'clutter' to get noticed.

"If your marketing is like everyone else's it just won't get noticed. And remember, you're not just competing with other businesses in your industry for your target market's attention – you're competing with every other type of business which is marketing to them.

"In reality that's a daunting prospect and explains why most marketing doesn't work – none of it rises above the clutter and 95% of it goes straight in the trash or simply isn't even noticed.

"So now you know why most marketing fails or never reaches the level it should. The message is wrong, the format is wrong and it never rises above the clutter. In many respects this last piece of the puzzle is the most important. You see, you can have the best message and format, but if no one notices it – it will still fail.

"That's why we advise you to look at what other people are doing with their marketing. Pay close attention to the types of media you've chosen to use to reach your target market. For example, if you're going to use lead generation letters, what formats do you receive through your own mail at home and at work that stand out for you? What gimmicks stand out? What letters ethically force you to respond? The chances are you can mimic and swipe these approaches and tailor them to your own business.

"But above all else don't be boring. You see, with marketing pieces that rise above the clutter, you put your business on a different level to all other businesses in your industry. You cannot underestimate the effect of being different with your marketing can have on your business.

"For instance, let's use the lead generation letter as an example. Most businesses will of course do their level best to write a professional letter. It won't include the right message but it's okay, and the format they choose is a basic two-page letter. Again that's fine. The problem is they send it in a plain white envelope, with the contact details printed on to a label (it's easier to do this – they think) and metered.

"They send this out and wonder why they didn't get a response. And it's simple. They could have been giving away $50 bills inside the envelope, but 99% of people didn't even open it. Why? Because it smacks of 'junk mail' and it looks like 95% of other marketing that arrives on their desk.

"You see, whether you like it or not, we all subconsciously have two piles in our mind when we're sorting mail. We have Pile A and Pile B. Pile A is stuff that looks uninteresting and like junk. It takes us approximately half a second to decide this. Yes, just half a second. Pile B, on the other hand, is stuff that looks interesting. Stuff that we will either open right now, or leave to open later. If your letter isn't on Pile B you've had it. That's why it needs to rise above the clutter and look interesting. Most letters unfortunately go on Pile A. They are doomed to failure just because of this.

"But now you know this, you can do something about it. The rule is simple. Never, ever, use a marketing piece that looks boring. Never, ever, use a marketing piece that looks like junk. Never, ever, use a marketing piece that doesn't rise above the clutter. Do this and we promise your results will astonish you."

Key Summary & Action Points

1. Getting results from your marketing pieces is difficult unless you ensure they have a complete message, use the right format and have stand-out appeal.

2. Never spend money on a marketing piece unless it adheres to (1) above, otherwise you might as well throw money down the toilet – you wouldn't do that, so don't do it with your marketing pieces.

Why Businesses Stop Growing...

9. How Do We Get More Referrals?

Introduction

You should now have a good understanding of the 5 Ms Of Marketing Your Business. To recap, here they are...

- <u>Market:</u> Who you are targeting (your 'Target Market').

- <u>Message:</u> Why someone should use your business rather than anyone else (your competitors) and what you need to convey in your message to get people to respond and buy.

- <u>Media:</u> The marketing channels you will use to deliver your message to the market (i.e. website, advertisements, direct mail, articles, etc.).

- <u>Moment:</u> Timing is everything!

- <u>Method:</u> What 'marketing piece' will you use for each media to rise above the clutter and get noticed over EVERY other business that's marketing to your target market (notice this is other direct competitors AND every other type of business trying to get your potential customers to buy from them).

These five core elements need to be the focus of your growth across the 4 Business Multipliers. Again to recap, here they are...

- Referral

- General Marketing

- Sales Conversion

- Maximizing Customer Value

So let's start with referral.

Our research has shown that 97% of business owners are dissatisfied with the volume of referrals they actually generate, whether through customers or other referral sources such as the banks, lawyers, IFAs and others. In other words, they believe they should do a whole lot better.

There are three significant reasons for this 'underachievement'...

- REASON #1: APATHY

  Most people simply don't recommend them because they have no cause to. The referral process for most businesses is a reactive one (people only ever suggest a supplier if they are asked. This is because they have no real reason to enthuse about their suppliers). Yes all good businesses get referrals, but customers need to have a reason and/or an incentive to recommend other people. We call the incentive a 'Customer Incentive Reward Program'.

  Putting in place a Customer Incentive Reward Program (alongside a Unique Perceived Benefit – we covered this when we discussed the message) which focuses on getting referrals is one of the easiest and most beneficial things you can do.

A structured Customer Incentive Reward Program when combined with your Unique Perceived Benefit will give your business the following benefits:

-   A constant supply of quality referrals.

-   Increased enthusiasm dealing with people who are highly interested in your products/services.

-   An increase in the quality of customers.

-   Increased profits. You spend less time and money converting referred people. They have already been recommended and therefore trust is already established.

-   As a result, referred people tend to value your products/services more than an 'ordinary' prospect. They usually don't 'shop around' to get the best price. This means you'll be able to sell your products/services at an optimum price (or at least at a good level).

-   An effective Customer Incentive Reward Program will help strengthen relationships with your customers. By helping their friends, colleagues and business associates, you make customers look good in the eyes of their peers.

IMPORTANT NOTE:

If you've tried a Customer Incentive Reward Program before without success (like many other businesses) there are two simple reasons why it probably didn't work as well as you had hoped: (1) see reason #2 below, and (2) because the marketing

---

pieces you used to promote the program weren't effective (see 'Method' above).

So please don't say to yourself – "We've tried this before and it didn't work – so I'm not trying it again". The simple fact is they DO work; you just have to know how to do it.

- REASON #2: NO DISCERNIBLE DIFFERENCE BETWEEN SUPPLIERS

  Just being good at what you do isn't sufficient. You see, as we've already discussed, most people think all suppliers are the same. Why would they recommend you to someone else when they think you and your competitors are identical?

- REASON #3: NO SYSTEM

  Research has shown that some two-thirds of customers say they are prepared to recommend their suppliers to others, but only 6% say they have ever been asked.

  That's a shocking statistic, but shows that most businesses just don't have any system in place for requesting referrals from customers. If you don't ask – you don't get.

The good news is there is a simple formula you can use to rapidly improve the number of referrals you get...

The Formula For Getting   A
        Constant Stream Of Referrals

(1) Good Business

+

(2) Referral System   +
(Customer Incentive Reward Program)   +

(4) Effective Communication Of Program

(3) Highly Sought-After Uniqueness   =

You need **ALL 4** elements of the formula to really motivate people to recommend you. If you're missing just one of these elements, then the number of referrals you get is significantly reduced.

Now, we're taking it for granted that you offer a good level of service to

Constant Stream Of Referrals   your customers,

therefore you need to focus on creating a 'highly sought-after uniqueness' (you should already have some thoughts about this as we discussed it earlier), together with a 'Customer Incentive Reward Program'.

Why Businesses Stop Growing...

A Customer Incentive Reward Program is literally the system you use to ensure ALL customers are aware that you want referrals, and the incentive can be anything from vouchers, money off their services, or anything you believe will incentivize your customers to give you more referrals. Experience has shown us that the more generous you are – the more you get.

One thing to think about with referrals and the incentives you offer customers is that a referral doesn't cost you anything to get.

Therefore, other than the cost of your incentive, your acquisition cost is ZERO. So you can 'afford' to spend more on the incentive to acquire the referral in the first place.

As we explained earlier, the 'highly sought-after uniqueness' is a more challenging element for you to create. You have to come up with something that's not only highly desired by your customers and potential customers, but something that your competitors don't offer. But hopefully you have some ideas on this already.

And finally you need an effective method to communicate the referral program to your customers.

What you need here is something that really stands out and ensures customers are motivated and excited about the program once they read or listen to your message.

It really is that simple. But as we explained, all three components are essential if you are looking to ramp up your referrals.

Black & Grey Widgets

At least Black & Grey are seriously thinking about how they can get more referrals. Like most businesses, they find themselves frustrated in the knowledge that they offer a good service to most, if not all customers, and it puzzles them why they don't get more.

They decide that the best way to get more referrals is to ask customers at the end of each customer meeting. That's better than nothing, and to a certain extent should generate a few more referrals.

But, because they don't have all the component parts of a successful referral system, they will still feel frustrated at the lack of success they achieve in this area, and even though they know they should be doing it, some people in the business still shy away from asking the question. But nevertheless, it's a step in the right direction.

Rainbow Widgets

"You see, you can't blame your customers for not giving you more referrals. If you don't have a system in place, you're leaving the growth of your business in this area down to fate. You have no control over the process and without a system you will never ever generate the level of referrals you feel you deserve.

"Once you've decided on your uniqueness, you can then agree what incentive you're going to use. Giving customers a gift or a voucher off their next purchase always work well.

"You just need to decide on what you believe will be the most attractive incentive to give your customers and then start promoting it to them, first by letter, and then by making sure at customer meetings it is an agenda item to discuss.

"This is your SYSTEM. Yes it's that simple. The key, like for everything we're telling you today, is to follow through!"

Key Summary & Action Points

1. You can increase your referrals as long as you put a SYSTEM in place.

2. Key to a successful referral system is to combine your uniqueness with a good incentive, and to then communicate it at every opportunity to customers.

10. How Do We Get More Customers From General Marketing Activities?

Introduction

"But Marketing Doesn't Work"

There is so much more business to be gained by proactively targeting the right businesses.

So why is it that many businesses shy away from using general marketing methods? We've discovered a few reasons...

1. Most people have tried a number of strategies, but because they got poor results, they conclude they don't work.

2. In most cases it's not that the strategy doesn't work – it's because the techniques used were poor – resulting in less than acceptable results.

3. Other methods such as telemarketing, seminars and articles (which are used with varying degrees of success by many businesses) would be significantly more successful with the right methodology.

IMPORTANT NOTE:

Reasons '2' and '3' above are caused by people NOT using the '5 Ms Of Marketing Your Business'.

But with the right execution and using the right approach you can get excellent results from many general marketing activities such as...

- Direct mail (letters, postcards, etc.) – Still by far THE best method for generating inquiries for virtually every business!

- Press Releases

- Special Reports/Articles

- Newspaper / Magazine Ads

- Classified Ads

- Yellow Pages Ads (yes, with the right ad, Yellow Pages advertising can still be successful for many businesses)

- Networking (with innovative thought-provoking scripts/presentations)

- Business Cards (not like conventional business cards)

- Websites

- Google AdWords

- Social Media (Facebook, etc.)

There are of course many other marketing activities you can use. The key is to use multiple strategies.

IMPORTANT NOTE ABOUT YOUR CHOICE OF GENERAL MARKETING ACTIVITIES

Our advice with every marketing activity you consider is to only use those that give you a return for the minimal time and effort. Even if something is 'FREE' (i.e. Facebook) there is still a cost – based on the time you put in. Time, or more accurately a lack of time, is the one thing that will restrict you in the growth of your business. So the more economical you are with your use of it and the more effective you become managing your time – the better.

You should therefore be choosing marketing activities which are kind to you in terms of the time you need to allocate to them and of course the return you get for your efforts.

Only you can decide what's right. But always be mindful of the trade-off you have to make.

The key, as we mentioned above, is to ensure you apply ALL '5 Ms of Marketing' to your general marketing activities. This is what gives you leverage. It's these 5 elements that add power to your 'marketing pieces' (the actual marketing piece that you use in each media – i.e. your actual advert, your website, your letter, etc.).

The 5 Ms are in essence what makes marketing work. Without them results are unsatisfactory, but with them – your success is virtually guaranteed!

Black & Grey Widgets

Black & Grey know they need to improve in this area. They know they need to be more active. They however, face the challenge most businesses face, in that they've never really had any success in this area, so they're starting from a blank piece of paper. They don't have a grasp of the 5 Ms so this immediately puts them at a disadvantage, but they're going to choose several activities and see how it goes.

Rainbow Widgets

"Hopefully you can see how everything is now starting to come together. Applying the 5 Ms to your general marketing activities will ensure your results exceed your expectations, but like everything we advise you to do, you should test before investing large sums in any activity.

"Remember, the big disadvantage you have when you've never used a marketing activity before – is you simply don't know how well it is going to work. Even when you're as experienced as we are, you still need to move forward with caution. We've seen many different businesses lose thousands of dollars, even tens of thousands of dollars, by deciding to go with a certain activity and pumping significant funds into it – only to realize it just doesn't work. It's too late by then. So our advice is to always test small. You can always increase your investment once you know what results your activities are generating.

"For example, let's say you're going to send a lead generation letter to your target market. There are 1,000 businesses in your target market. Let's say, because you've heeded our advice, your letter stands out and as a result your cost including postage works out at, say, $3.00 per letter. The less experienced person would then eagerly mail all 1,000 businesses at a cost of $3,000. The more experienced would mail, say, 200 each of two different versions, at a cost of $1,200, and wait to analyze the results before moving forward and mailing the rest.

"Testing two different versions (having changed just one variable such as the headline) will bring you two different results. Let's say letter 1 generated 1 reply and letter 2 generated 3 replies. In other words, letter 2 generated 300% more inquiries (not uncommon when you test). Now we can mail the last 600 with letter 2 which will yield a further 9 replies, totaling 13 responses – not bad. However, if we'd just mailed letter 1 to the 1000 businesses, we'd have only received 5 responses – yet our total costs would be the same.

"Testing is therefore another way to leverage your marketing and the corresponding results. It's how smart marketers always roll out their marketing, especially when they're trying something new.

"Probably the biggest area where most businesses make this mistake is with their website. Several hundred or several thousand dollars are often spent creating a site with bells and whistles on. It looks great but doesn't generate any tangible results.

"So we advise you to be pragmatic with all your marketing spend, until you have concrete results. Yes this process takes longer, but it's by far the most sensible way to grow your business, and in the long run, will not only help you save thousands of dollars, it will help you generate significantly better results as long as you test.

"In terms of the marketing activities you should use, we've detailed these earlier, but by far the best method is to use direct mail. Even though most businesses conclude direct mail doesn't work, when you apply the 5 Ms your results will surprise you and occasionally will astonish you."

Key Summary & Action Points

1. You are seriously hindering your growth if you don't use general marketing activities.

2. As long as you apply the 5 Ms to your general marketing activities, there's no reason why you can't achieve at least moderate success.

3. For activities which you've never used before, make sure you test small and only invest more heavily once you know it works.

4. When testing, only change one variable at a time. If you change more than one, you'll never know which variable worked.

10. More Customers From General Marketing

11. How Do We Convert More Inquiries Into Good Customers?

Introduction

As we've discovered, many business owners spend a considerable amount of time, energy and money in order to generate inquiries.

However, there's little point generating dozens of inquiries each month from referral and general marketing activities if you only convert a small percentage of them – it's a huge missed opportunity!

The process of converting inquiries into customers is called 'Sales Conversion' and is the third Business Multiplier.

As soon as an inquiry is created (either from your referral or general marketing activities), you need to have a 'SYSTEM' (yes, a system!) in order to convert as many as you can into good-quality customers.

Concentrating more on converting inquiries into customers will ensure two things:

1. You'll rapidly transform the business

2. You'll maximize the return on investment the business makes on ALL its referral and general marketing strategies

The good news is that putting in place a system to convert more inquiries into customers costs very little (if anything at all) and the results are instant!

So what is a Sales Conversion System?

In simple terms a sales conversion system is a system used to ensure the business generates more customers from the number of inquiries generated.

It starts the moment the inquiry is received, and continues right through to the point when that inquiry becomes a customer.

One of the HUGE hidden benefits of a successful system is that the process of converting inquiries is driven by the system, rather than the individual – which means anyone (with the right experience in the business) can use the system to great effect.

Here's a simple diagram explaining why you need a sales conversion system...

The Effect Of Positive Contacts In The Sales Cycle

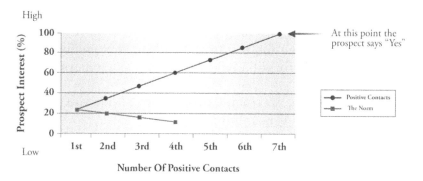

The Norm – By the fourth contact the prospect's interest is lower than where it started. They are now further away from the sale! That's why 90% of sales people have given up!

Positive Contacts – By the fourth contact the prospect's interest is high. Now it's only a matter of time and a couple more positive contacts before the sale is made.

What this chart shows is that the prospect must reach a certain level of interest before he or she is prepared to say "Yes" and buy your product or service.

Therefore, what you need to do is increase the prospect's interest each time the business makes contact with them. A contact can be a meeting, a letter, a fax, an e-mail – or any way in which you make contact with prospects.

Research has shown that on average it takes 7 positive contacts ('The Rule of 7') before the prospect says, "Yes".

A sales conversion system should therefore automatically cater to these contacts, which in turn will increase the chances of getting a positive result with the vast majority of prospects.

Your sales conversion system should focus on each stage and as a result many more inquiries will turn into customers.

...and there's one more important piece of the jigsaw to consider. We call it the 'Follow-Up Ladder'.

You see, Follow-Up is not practiced by many businesses (think about it, how many positive contacts do you have at the moment from the inquiry to the sale?). This means those that follow up correctly will always gain more customers.

To reinforce this point further, we think you'll find these research results very interesting...

• A recent study conducted by Performark (a research company in the USA) showed how few companies follow up properly or even at all.

They found that out of 10,000 advertising inquiries – 22% never received the information they requested, 45% received the information more than 65 days after their request, for 12% it took more than 120 days to receive their information, and 87% were never contacted by a sales representative.

- A recent study by Thomas Publishing Company showed that most salespeople give up too early, regardless of the industry.

According to the study, 80% of sales to businesses are made on the fifth sales call, but only 10% of salespeople call more than three times (the diagram on page 105 shows the complete details of the study).

- A recent study conducted by Tom Rayfield, a UK direct marketing expert, showed that companies are very poor at follow-up. Taking 200 randomly selected advertisers, he replied to them all to measure follow-up responses.

To his amazement, the average time taken for people to reply to him was eight days, and 17 companies (8.5%) didn't even bother to reply!

- Dr. Geoffrey Lant, the renowned marketing and research consultant, reasons that most buying decisions are made after seven contacts over an 18-month period. He calls this the 'Rule of 7', and many more studies support this.

What you need to do is make a positive impression on the prospect at each contact. By doing this, you speed up the sales cycle and keep more prospects in it – resulting in more sales.

If one of your contacts has a less than positive impact on your prospect, their interest drops, making it harder for you to close the sale. This is a basic but very important tactic for you to apply and understand. The diagram on the next page shows how it all fits together...

When Do Prospects Turn Into Buyers?

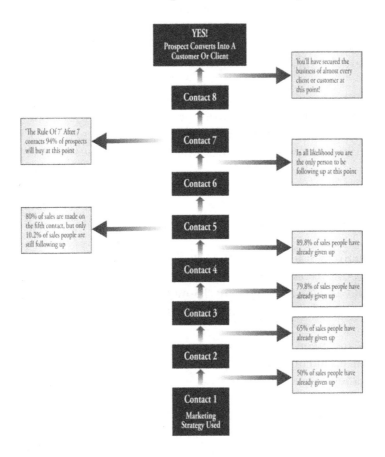

Data based on Thomas Publishing
Company research findings

Why A Sales Conversion System Is So Powerful, And Why Your Business Must Have One

Let's just take this hypothetical situation...

Let's say, at the moment, you convert 20% of general marketing inquiries into customers. The average sale is $1,000, and 10 inquiries are generated each month. Look at the table below and see the effect a sales conversion system can have on the business in just 12 months:

Conversion Rate	Inquiries Per Month	Customers Per Month	Average Order ($)	Annual Sales ($)
20%	10	2	1000	24,000
30%	10	3	1000	36,000
40%	10	4	1000	48,000
50%	10	5	1000	60,000

Improving the sales conversion rate from 20% - 30% results in a growth of 50%. Doubling the sales conversion rate from 20% - 40% results in a 100% growth in new business. That's why a sales conversion process is so powerful and so important.

By the way, if you think it's difficult to improve the conversion from 20% to 40%, or 30% to 60%, or more – it isn't!

...and remember, improving the sales conversion rate is achieved **without any extra cost**. And that's the beauty of it!

Black & Grey Widgets

Black & Grey recognize that they could do better with their inquiry conversion. However, they feel content in the knowledge that for referrals they convert at around 60%.

What they fail to recognize is their conversion of general marketing inquiries is lower – much lower, and if they decide to increase their prices (which is on the agenda) their conversion of referral inquiries will also plummet.

Like most businesses, Black & Grey give little thought to how they can improve their conversion rate, so it will be interesting to see how they do in the coming months!

Rainbow Widgets

"So putting in a sales conversion system gives you real leverage. You don't need any fancy software or any complicated system. You just need to plan each contact so the prospect gets wowed each time.

"For example, one of the points of contact that is almost always very weak is parking for the prospect when they arrive for a meeting. Even if you have no on-site parking there are many things that can be done to make this part of the system a real positive experience for the prospect.

"You're lucky you do have on-site parking, but we noticed as we arrived that it was full. We parked at a pay parking lot 5 minutes walk away. We're pretty sure that's also the experience prospects have when they come to meet you. So now we've brought this to your attention, what can you do to make parking a real wow moment for the prospect?

"You see, because so few businesses really look at the detail of these points of contact, it's easy to score big points against them, especially when you're in competition with them. The likelihood that they have also thought carefully about these contact points is remote – so you win and you win big.

"It's these points of contact and how well you administer them that set apart the good from the great. More importantly, when you look to increase your prices, this makes a big difference to your conversion. So a sales conversion system will give you the ability to convert more inquiries (referral and general marketing) into customers and at the right price, all with zero cost.

"Plus, there's a number of what we call 'sales conversion strategies' that really help to convert the prospect. For example, Marketing Assets such as guarantees, sales barrier demolition, and social proof are excellent 'sales converters' that again cost nothing to apply.

"That's the sort of leverage any business would love – and you can get it instantly."

Key Summary & Action Points

1. A sales conversion system is a series of positive contact points and sales conversion strategies you put in place to increase the interest and desire of the prospect, taking them closer and closer to the sale.

2. An effective sales conversion system costs virtually nothing to put in place and the effects are gained instantly.

---

12. How Do We Increase Customer Value?

Introduction

We can go into almost any business and release thousands of dollars of revenue and profit, literally overnight. We can do this NOT because we're expert marketers and financial wizards, but because we tap into 'The Acres Of Diamonds Principle' that every business possesses.

So what is this 'Acres Of Diamonds Principle'? Let us explain...

One of the most interesting Americans who lived in the 19th century was a man by the name of Russell Herman Conwell. He was born in 1843 and lived until 1925. He was a lawyer for about fifteen years until he became a clergyman.

One day, a young man went to him and told him he wanted a college education but couldn't swing it financially. Dr. Conwell decided, at that moment, what his aim in life was – besides being a man of the cloth, that is. He decided to build a university for unfortunate, but deserving, students. He did have a challenge, however. He would need a few million dollars to build the university. For Dr. Conwell, and anyone with real purpose in life, nothing could stand in the way of his goal.

Several years before this incident, Dr. Conwell was tremendously intrigued by a true story – with its ageless moral. The story was about a farmer who lived in Africa and through a visitor became tremendously excited about looking for diamonds.

Diamonds were already discovered in abundance on the African continent and this farmer got so excited about the idea of millions of dollars worth of diamonds that he sold his farm to head out to the diamond line.

He wandered all over the continent, as the years slipped by, constantly searching for diamonds and wealth, which he never found. Eventually he went completely broke and threw himself into a river and drowned.

Meanwhile, the new owner of his farm picked up an unusual-looking rock about the size of a country egg and put it on his mantle as a sort of curiosity.

A visitor stopped by and, viewing the rock, practically went into terminal convulsions.

He told the new owner of the farm that the funny-looking rock on his mantle was about the biggest diamond that had ever been found. The new owner of the farm said, "Heck, the whole farm is covered with them" – and sure enough it was.

The farm turned out to be the Kimberley Diamond Mine...the richest the world has ever known. The original farmer was literally standing on 'Acres of Diamonds' until he sold his farm.

Dr. Conwell learned from the story of the farmer and continued to teach its moral. Each of us is right in the middle of our own 'Acre of Diamonds', if only we would realize it and develop the ground we are standing on before charging off in search of greener pastures.

Dr. Conwell told this story many times and attracted enormous audiences. He told the story long enough to raise the money to start the college for underprivileged, deserving students. In fact, he raised nearly six million dollars and the university he founded, Temple University in Philadelphia, has at least ten degree-granting colleges and six other schools.

When Dr. Russell H. Conwell talked about each of us being right on our own 'Acre of Diamonds', he meant it. This story does not get old...it will be true forever... Opportunity does not just come along – it is there all the time – we just have to see it.

So how does this relate to you and your business?

Well, by far and away the most lucrative part of your business is your customers...

It's the customers who are your own 'Acres Of Diamonds'.

Once a new customer is acquired it's your 'duty' to provide them with more value, more service and more benefits.

This is known as 'Back-End Selling'.

Therefore you need to put in place a system for increasing the monetary value of each customer to you. There are just 3 key areas to focus on...

1. Customer Retention
2. Increasing Fees/Prices
3. Selling More Products/Services

Let's take a look at each one...

1. Customer Retention

Although many businesses believe they don't have a problem with retention, it's fair to say that if they could still retain a few of those who DO leave each year, it will amount to a significant sum over time.

A more accurate view for many businesses would be to say that they don't have a retention problem today.

Why Businesses Stop Growing...

For a start, all customers will eventually retire, sell, die or go bust. Secondly, most customers don't move simply because they don't perceive that they have better options. In other words, businesses keep customers because the competition hasn't got their marketing act together. <u>This is changing!</u>

The good news is there are some very simple strategies to follow, which have a major impact on your retention of customers....

Proven strategies that help improve retention are...

- Unique Competitive Advantage (we've already covered this earlier)

- Moments Of Truth (see below)

- Managing Your Customer Base (see below)

Moments Of Truth

So let's first look at Moments Of Truth and how you can use it to transform how you work with your customers...

Moments Of Truth goes to the heart of growing your business in this new economy. We're going to explain how you can transform the experience every customer has with you – so they not only stay with you for longer, but they also refer you more frequently and are much less resistant to any fee or price increases.

This added value approach may sound hard to believe, but in the next few minutes you'll see for yourself just how powerful Moments Of Truth can be.

So what exactly is Moments Of Truth? Let us explain...

In 1987 Jan Carlzon, the CEO of Scandinavian Airlines, wrote the book, 'Moments Of Truth'. It explained how he took the airline from deficit to profit by 'moving' the airline to a customer-focused organization.

Now, as you know, there have been many books written on customer service, but where this book and Carlzon's strategies really differ, is his focus on each interaction the customer has with the business. He calls these 'Moments of Truth' and, of course, each interaction can be a positive or a negative experience.

Scandinavian Airlines prospered because they worked very hard to make sure each Moment Of Truth with their customers was a very positive experience and the results they achieved were a testament to this.

Take a look at the diagram on the next page. It shows how at each contact (Moment Of Truth) you need to ensure each interaction is a favorable one for your customers.

Moments Of Truth Explained...

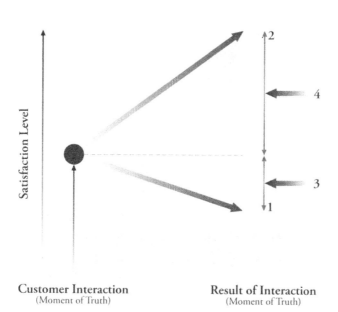

Customer Interaction
(Moment of Truth)

Result of Interaction
(Moment of Truth)

Legend:

1.   The effect on the customer using traditional marketing strategies. Notice the Moment Of Truth was a negative experience reducing the customer's satisfaction – and therefore creating discontent with an existing customer.

2.   Moments Of Truth Approach. By breaking down each step **even further** the interest level and satisfaction level is raised even higher.

3.   Shows the drop in interest level and satisfaction using traditional techniques (or none at all).

4.   Shows the increase gained by using Moments Of Truth techniques.

Therefore what you need to do is increase the satisfaction level of each customer when any contact occurs (Moment Of Truth).

A contact can be a meeting, a letter, a fax, an e-mail – or any way in which your business comes into contact with a customer.

To explain this point further, and just in case you have any doubts about the power of Moments Of Truth and the effect it can have on your business, here's a great example of how any industry can capitalize on this fabulous strategy...

Harvey Mackay (author of 'Swim With The Sharks Without Being Eaten Alive') tells a wonderful story about a cab driver that demonstrates Moments Of Truth perfectly...

He was waiting in line for a ride at the airport.

When a cab pulled up, the first thing Harvey noticed was that the taxi was polished to a bright shine.

Smartly dressed in a white shirt, black tie and freshly pressed black trousers, the cab driver jumped out and rounded the car to open the back passenger door for Harvey.

He handed Harvey a laminated card and said:

"I'm Wally, your driver. While I'm loading your bags in the trunk I'd like you to read my mission statement."

Taken aback, Harvey read the card. It said: Wally's Mission Statement:

> 'To get my customers to their destination in the quickest, safest and cheapest way possible in a friendly environment.'

This blew Harvey away. Especially when he noticed that the inside of the cab matched the outside. Spotlessly clean!

As he slid behind the wheel, Wally said, "Would you like a cup of coffee? I have a thermos of regular and one of decaf."

Harvey said jokingly, "No, I'd prefer a soft drink."

Wally smiled and said, "No problem. I have a cooler upfront with regular and Diet Coke, water and orange juice."

Almost stuttering, Harvey said, "I'll take a Diet Coke."

Handing him his drink, Wally said, "If you'd like something to read, I have The Wall Street Journal, Time, Sports Illustrated and USA Today."

As they were pulling away, Wally handed Harvey another laminated card.

"These are the stations I get and the music they play, if you'd like to listen to the radio."

And, as if that wasn't enough, Wally told Harvey that he had the air conditioning on and asked if the temperature was comfortable for him.

Then he advised Harvey of the best route to his destination for that time of day.

He also let him know that he'd be happy to chat and tell him about some of the sights, or if Harvey preferred, to leave him with his own thoughts.

Then Harvey said, "Tell me Wally, have you always served customers like this?"

Wally smiled into the rear-view mirror. "No, not always. In fact, it's only been in the last two years. My first five years driving, I spent most of my time complaining like all the rest of the cabbies do.

"Then I decided to do things differently. I looked around at the other cabs and their drivers. The cabs were dirty, the drivers were unfriendly and the customers were unhappy. So I decided to make some changes. I put in a few at a time. When my customers responded well, I did more."

"I take it that has paid off for you," Harvey said.

"It sure has," Wally replied. "In my first year I doubled my income from the previous year. This year I'll probably quadruple it. You were lucky to get me today. I don't sit at cabstands anymore.

"My customers call me for appointments on my cell phone or leave a message on my answering machine. If I can't pick them up myself I get a reliable cabbie friend to do it, and I take a piece of the action."

Wally was implementing Moments Of Truth, even though he didn't realize it!

This true story shows if Moments Of Truth can be so successful for a cab driver – it can work for any type of business – <u>ESPECIALLY YOUR BUSINESS</u>!

So how can you use this to your advantage? There are just three simple steps. Let's take a look at each one...

Step 1: Identify The Key Interactions (Moments) You Have With Your Customers

Simply identify every single interaction you have with your customers. Here are the main ones...

- Car Parking (when a customer comes to your office/showroom/retail store/restaurant, etc.)

- Meetings At Customer's Home Or Place Of Work

- Reception Area

- Meeting Room(s)

- Telephone Answering

- E-Mail

- General Correspondence

- Complaint Handling And Procedures

Step 2: Create And Systemize The Positive Experience At Each Moment

Now all you do is look at how you can maximize the interaction so that customers have a very positive experience with you at each interaction.

Step 3: Now Add 'Special' Moments Of Truth

What Moments Of Truth focuses on is the 'normal' interactions you have with your customers. The final piece of the jigsaw is to introduce NEW Moments Of Truth that heighten the experience for the prospect or customer.

Here's a good example...

The Radisson chain of hotels is excellent at including 'Special' Moments Of Truth in the customer experience. Let's compare their approach to receiving new customers with the 'standard' service of other good hotels...

Moment Of Truth	Good Hotels	The Radisson
Check-In	Prompt, courteous welcome and efficient checking in.	Prompt, courteous welcome and efficient checking in, plus an acknowledgement that this is your first visit and a complimentary

		upgrade.
Entry Into Room	Maybe a complimentary bowl of fruit, bottle of water and a welcome message on the TV screen.	Welcome message on TV screen. A chocolate dessert with your name written in the chocolate sauce saying 'Welcome <Name>'. A book entitled 'This Is My Favorite...' with the favorite recipes from 100 of the UK's best chefs – and a complimentary note sticking out of the top saying: 'Dear <Name>, We believe this is your first visit to the Hotel. Please accept this book with our compliments.' And finally a 'Welcome Card' from the Hotel Manager, personally addressed.

These are just two Moments Of Truth – but as you can see, by adding 'Special' Moments Of Truth to the experience, you really do set yourself apart!

Once you've tackled the more obvious points of contact, you don't have to stop there. Moments of Truth is all about focusing your business on the expectations of your customers.

Why Businesses Stop Growing...

So the question is – what 'Special Moments Of Truth' can you build into the business when serving prospects and customers?

Managing Your Customer Base

This final method to help retain more customers is, once again, extremely effective once you apply it to your business.

Managing your customer base is simple as long as you realize that not all customers are the same. Look at this table.

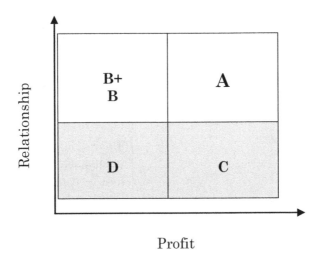

Profit

We are going to use this 'Boston Matrix' diagram to analyze your own customer base.

The x-axis represents the financial value that the customer has to your business. The further along the axis, the more profitable they are. The y-axis measures the intangible, how much you enjoy having them as a customer. The further up the scale, the better the relationship with them, and the greater respect they have for your staff and your business as a whole.

With these four boxes you can now very easily categorize your customers...

Those in Box A are your best customers, very profitable for you and enjoyable to work with.

Those in Box B are the bread-and-butter customers. They are perfectly pleasant to work with, but don't make as much profit for you as you would wish. Within this group are the B+s.

These are customers that you earmark as having potential. They don't spend enough with you yet but given the right handling, they could become A customers.

Box C holds an odd breed. As profitable as A customers but unpleasant to deal with. These are the people who everyone dreads picking up the phone to. These are the ones who make your heart sink when you send the bill out because you know what's coming next – the complaint. In some cases they may be polite and friendly with you, but bully your staff.

Box D is even worse. Not only are they nasty to deal with but you don't make enough money on them either!

In most businesses Box B is the most heavily populated, together with (hopefully) a reasonable number in Box A. Box C may have the odd one with any number lurking in Box D.

The problem with this set-up is that those in boxes C & D, while numerically in the minority, demand an unwarranted amount of your resources.

Their demands, lack of support and cooperation, complaints and general negativity drain your time and profit. As a result the 'nice' people in B and A, who don't jump up and down and pester you, are in danger of getting neglected. The focus of the business ends up too much on those below the line.

The solution is to treat each box differently. Let us show you what we mean.

Managing Your Customers

Let's start with Box D. You don't like them, they don't like you and you're not happy with the sales value they generate. Why are they still in <u>your</u> business? Having identified them, we can now remove them.

But, like any cull, this should be a controlled process that works to your advantage. Decide who goes when, in order to minimize the impact on your cash flow. Even look to sell them to a competitor!

Ensure that any 'firing' letters are inoffensive and diplomatic to avoid the wrong message getting out in to the market place.

Crucially though, commit to removing all D customers.

Remember that the only difference between C and D customers is the profit that you make. That, at least, earns C customers the chance of a reprieve.

Meet with them, explain why the relationship isn't working for you and try to get to the root of the problem. Satisfactory resolution could mean another A customer. No resolution means another D customer to be handled out of the business. No one stays in the C box.

How different does the business look now that we only have A and B (and B+) customers to look after? We've raised morale and freed up a significant amount of time. Now we can look after our customers properly.

The business can now focus its time on your A customers, ensuring their retention, increasing referrals and maximizing customer value. In addition it can work with the B+s, nurturing their growth.

Let's not forget that the B customers are in the majority, and while nice people and easy customers to manage, they are not as profitable as we would wish.

The answer, therefore, is to ensure that they are predominantly looked after by a systemized process that meets their needs, and is more effective at the sales value their budget allows.

2. Increasing Fees/Prices

One of the goals of your business should be to increase your prices. No other strategy will be able to give you increased profit margins so quickly.

However, the only way you can increase your prices is by providing ADDED VALUE to your customers.

In our experience, many businesses charge too little for their products or services.

There are only two factors to consider when setting your prices – value and profit. Concentrate on giving extraordinary levels of value – and profit will take care of itself!

There are two key factors to consider. Let's take a look at them...

Pricing & Adding Value

So how do you charge the right price for your products or services and how do you increase your prices by adding more value than the competition – ideally without having to change anything in your business?

At the outset this may seem difficult and quite challenging (and daunting), but once you understand how price and value work in harmony, and what you can do to ethically use it to your advantage, you'll be surprised at how easy it really is.

So let's first look at how to charge the perfect price for your products or services...

How To Charge The Perfect Price For Your Products Or Services

We can quite confidently say that you are **not** charging the right price (high enough) for your products or services. And when you consider that increasing your prices is *the quickest and easiest way to grow any business* with increased profits, you're missing out on a huge opportunity.

Here's how most businesses go about pricing their products or services...

- They look at what their competitors charge.

- They decide 'where' they want their customers to view them (or what the customer will stand) – are they 'low priced', 'middle of the road' or 'high end'?

- They then price their products or services based on the results of the two scenarios above but with market influence being dominant.

This is what's known as 'price positioning' and to a certain extent it does serve a purpose. But what it means is the business bases their own prices on where they see themselves positioned in the market, in relation to what their competitors charge.

You might be saying to yourself, "Well, that's fine – isn't that how pricing should be done?" No it isn't!

This is a fundamental mistake.

People rarely buy on price. Sure, there are a small percentage of people who buy the cheapest, but they are in the minority. Generally people buy based on 'VALUE', and 'price' and 'value' are two very different things!

Let us explain...

As a rule, people will automatically value your products or services more if they are priced higher. The opposite is also true!

This may surprise you, but think about this simple example...

You go to two different restaurants on two different nights...

The first restaurant has a low-priced menu. Although you may think, "Great, a cheap meal", you will start having doubts about the quality of the food and the service – even before you enter the restaurant.

You keep these doubts hidden until you wait ten minutes to be greeted. You pass this off as "one of those things" but your doubts are starting to come to the forefront.

You are seated at your table.

The table is still dirty from the previous diners. The waitress comes and takes your order. She has to keep asking you to repeat what you wanted. You really are now worrying. Not surprisingly, your order comes and it's all wrong, and so on.

The point here is, as soon as you saw the menu the doubts started, purely because the price was low. If you had a good experience then you'd be surprised, and you'd definitely go back.

The second point here is this – the restaurant should charge more if they serve you well and you have an enjoyable experience (the value is greater!).

The second restaurant you go to is different – very different...

The menu is very expensive. In fact, you've never been to a restaurant with prices so high. However, you automatically think, "It must be good if they charge these prices."

As long as you are treated exceptionally well and your food is also excellent, you would never question the bill. The point is that, as soon as you saw the prices, you perceived the restaurant to be good even before you entered!

If you had a bad experience you'd never go back and pay those prices. The point here is this – although the restaurant charged high prices, they demonstrated to you with their service and food why they charge high prices. IN OTHER WORDS, THE VALUE THEY PROVIDED AT THE VERY LEAST MATCHED YOUR EXPECTATIONS.

It's exactly the same with your pricing. If you charge too low, your prospects and customers will automatically think you can't be that good. On the other hand, if you charge high prices you'd better make sure customers receive excellent value – because that's what they'll expect.

The Big Question: How Do You Add Value?

When you add the principle of 'value' to pricing, this is when you build 'elasticity' into your prices, which means you have a greater flexibility in your pricing. Here's an important note about 'value' and how it links to price...

The Ultimate Principle On Value And Price

As long as you provide excellent value – people will flock to your business and pay handsomely for the privilege.

People often make the mistake of thinking that price is the main issue in the mind of their prospects or customers.

But what they're missing is this: if everyone is viewed by the prospect as 'the same' – i.e. companies don't take the time or effort to differentiate themselves from others and add considerable value – the only way the prospect can choose is based on price.

But when you add so much value to the business – substantially more than your competitors – you leave the prospect with little choice.

And often they'll pay much more than anyone else. Why? Because you've added so much value!

Also, when a customer decides to leave and turn to one of your competitors, they'll often say, 'Your price/fees are too high.' BUT WHAT THEY'RE REALLY SAYING IS THIS...

'Your products or services are not worth what you charge. I'm just not getting value for money!'

There's a big difference!

The following diagrams show the effect of value on price...

1. As you can see below, we have two similar but competing businesses – Business A and Business B. Let's say that

Why Businesses Stop Growing...

Business A is a competitor and Business B is YOUR business...

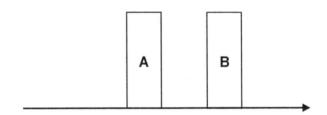

2. Let's assume that each business has a similar price structure for its products or services and similar value attached to them...

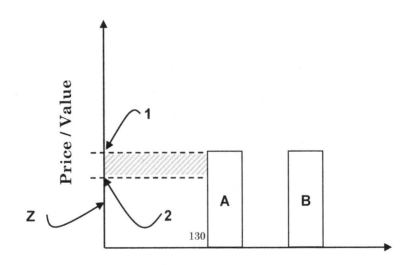

So at the moment point '1' (shown above) is the maximum value of each product or service offered by each business. So if we look at pricing either product or service, we are unlikely to get many sales if we price the products or services above point '1' because the perceived value is lower than the price.

But if we set the price at, say, point '2' we'd get more sales because now there is what we call 'added value' – the difference between the value (point 1) and the price (point 2). The shaded area represents the added value. Agreed?

So Business A may take the view it wants to compete heavily on price and therefore reduces its prices even further to, say, point 'Z' in an effort to capture more customers.

That represents the situation with every business and demonstrates the maximum prices they can charge – agreed?

Okay, so how can we make the price more ELASTIC? In other words, how can we increase the price range you can charge customers?

3. That's right – we add more value. How do you think we can add more value WITHOUT changing your business or even the products or services you offer? Quite simply we add the following (all but the first two are Marketing Assets)...

- Target Market

- Moments Of Truth

- Unique Competitive Advantage

- Benefits

- Irresistible Offer

- Headlines

- Guarantee/Risk Reversal

- Social Proof

These elements are at point 'C' on the diagram below. Now let's see how our diagram looks...

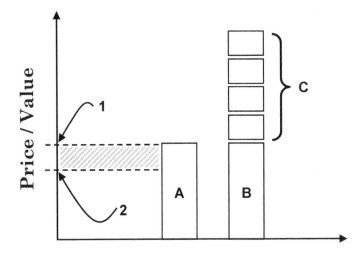

As you can see, we're adding value over and above what the competition are doing.

Now look at the price elasticity (3 – see diagram below). You could price your products or services right up to point 4 now. But would you get many sales at point 4? No you wouldn't, because at that point there's no added value. But what if you priced your services at point 5 – would you get many sales? Yes you would.

That's the power of adding value and creating price elasticity.

4. So what about a price-sensitive market? We explained earlier why, in most circumstances, a price-sensitive market isn't actually the case. But let's say at the moment you don't want (or you're nervous) to increase your prices because you believe you're in a price-sensitive market (or the economy is holding you back!).

So all you do is keep your prices the same. But now, after adding all this value, who do you think gets most of the sales? That's right – YOU do. Why? Because point 6 (see below) represents the added value your business (B) has over the competition (A).

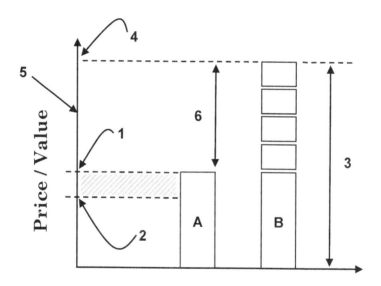

So that's how you can increase your prices, or maintain your existing prices, and STILL generate more customers and sales just by using the Marketing Assets, Target Market and Moments Of Truth to add value to your business.

Base your pricing on *value* rather than on price and you'll be surprised how much more money you'll make!

3. Selling More Products/Services

Now we need to get your customers buying more frequently from you. In other words – getting them to buy more products or services from you.

Here's why most businesses struggle to effectively sell more to their existing customers...

1. **NOT PACKAGED RIGHT:** The business tells the customer what the product or service is but it's not 'packaged' correctly, making it hard to buy and less appealing.

2. **NO ADDED VALUE:** Just as we have highlighted above, there is no added value communicated to the customer.

3. **NO OFFER:** When the products or services are offered to customers there's no offer making them irresistible to buy.

4. **NOT SOLD:** Remember when selling – you must adhere to the 5 Ms Of Marketing Your Business.

5. **MISSED OPPORTUNITIES:** The opportunities to sell your products or services are all around you, yet are often missed because you and your staff just don't 'see them'.

So, it's hardly surprising that selling more to existing customers generates a small percentage of the overall revenue in most businesses – yet the opposite should be true – and can be if you focus on all these elements.

Black & Grey Widgets

Black & Grey of course fully appreciate the impact a small increase in prices can have on their profits. So they decide to increase prices by 10% for the next 12 months. This is a good strategy. However, because they aren't adding value, this increase (although relatively easy with new customers) is likely to be met with disdain from a number of existing customers. How can they justify the increase?

Rainbow Widgets

"Moving to a value-based business is by far the best and easiest way to maximize sales and to increase profits. Retaining customers, increasing prices and selling more to existing customers are the three things you can focus on to increase the monetary value of every customer.

"Yes it takes time to put all these strategies into practice, but once they're in place they will keep working for you month after month.

"Once again, the great thing about all these strategies is they cost very little to apply and they work immediately once they're in place."

Key Summary & Action Points

1. To maximize the monetary value of your customers you have to focus on just three key areas: (1) Improving Customer Retention, (2) Increasing Prices/Fees and (3) Selling More Products/Services To Existing Customers.

2. To improve customer retention you need to create your unique competitive advantage, apply Moments Of Truth and manage your customer base effectively.

3. To increase prices you have to add value.

4. To sell more products or services you have to...

- package your products or services so they're more attractive to your customers

- add value

- create an enticing offer

- use the 5 Ms Of Marketing Your Business

- grasp the opportunities

13. Actions & Implementation Plan

Introduction

The first 12 agenda points cover the steps you need to take to quickly grow your business. This section looks at the actions you need to take and the implementation process.

Just like any board meeting, if the actions agreed at the meeting aren't carried out – the business won't move forward. The same can be said about this book.

It's taking action (massive action) that will get you the results you seek. So in this section we look at everything that needs to be put in place across the '5 Ms Of Marketing Your Business' and the '4 Business Multipliers'. The details on how you carry out each task have been shown throughout the book.

Actions – 5 Ms Of Marketing Your Business

Market

- Analyze your existing customer base. Look for the type of customers that generate 60-80% of your sales. These are the low-hanging fruit and represent the easiest customers to acquire.

- Look for specific target markets that you already have expertise in. The more credibility and social proof in these markets you have, the better.

- Use the target market characteristics detailed earlier. These will help you identify the best target market(s) for your business.

- Again, using the target market characteristics, write down clearly the definition of your target market(s).

Message

- Create your own Unique Perceived Benefit (unique competitive advantage). Remember, it not only has to be unique, it also has to be highly desired by your customers and potential customers (the target market).

- Convert all the features of your products or services and the delivery of them into benefits. People buy on emotion (benefits) and back up their decision with logic (features).

- Create an offer that's irresistible to your target market. Free Special Reports help position you as an expert and immediately set you apart from the competition. If relevant, you must 'sell' the meeting so the prospect is excited and more than happy to spend time with you.

- Every message and marketing piece must have a headline that grabs the attention of the target market. Your company name is NOT a headline.

- Create a number of powerful guarantees that minimize the risk customers take when using your products or services. Guarantees are also excellent sales converting strategies.

- Establish a sales barrier demolition to further differentiate your business and attract the target market to you like a magnet.

- Once you've created an irresistible offer together with your guarantee and sales barrier demolition, you need to list the reasons why you are making these things available. Otherwise the target market will believe what you're offering is too good to be true.

- The more proof and credibility you provide as part of your message – the more customers you'll acquire. You can't have enough testimonials and other sources of credibility.

- People are silently begging to be led. Therefore you must tell them what to do. You achieve this with what we call a call to action.

Media

- Select your media categories (Published Media, Direct Marketing Media, E-Media) to deliver your message to the target market. Tests have proved that combining all three media categories gets the best results.

Moment

- People are constantly moving 'in' and 'out' of buying mode because of their ever-changing circumstances. You use this to your advantage by contacting the target market at least twelve times a year (but the more the better). Therefore you need to create at least 12 marketing pieces a year to communicate your message to the target market.

Method

- Identifying your media categories will help you decide on your marketing pieces to use to deliver your message to the target market. To get results, your marketing pieces need to stand out and rise above the clutter. Remember, you are not just competing against direct competitors looking to acquire your target market; you are also competing against EVERY other business targeting the same people. The marketing pieces that

grab attention are the ones that get looked at –
increasing your chances of success considerably.

Actions – The 4 Practice Multipliers

More Inquiries By Referral

- Create a referral system for customers. For the system
  to work effectively you need a sought-after unique
  competitive advantage, an incentive and an effective
  method for communicating the referral system. Without
  all these things in place your referral system won't be as
  successful as it should be.

More Inquiries By General Marketing

- Having identified the media categories you'll be using to
  reach your target market, you should have a list of a
  number of general marketing activities you should be
  undertaking. You now need to create each marketing
  piece ready for launch. Remember to monitor the results
  of all your marketing and test small when you have no
  history of results.

Converting More Inquiries Into Sales (Sales Conversion)

- Create and apply a sales conversion system which helps
  you to convert more inquiries into customers. It should
  consist of at least 7 points of contact (most people buy
  after 7 contacts) and include sales conversion strategies
  such as guarantees and social proof (testimonials, etc.).

Maximizing Prices/Fees From Customers

- Improve your customer retention by (1) applying
  Moments Of Truth across your business and (2)
  managing your customer base by segmenting customers
  into the 5 key categories (A, B, B+, C, D).

- Increase prices by adding value.

- Sell more products or services by (1) making each of your products or services more desirable (packaging them so they are more appealing), (2) adding value, (3) creating a compelling offer for each product or service that makes it difficult for customers to refuse (use the 5 Ms for each product or service) and (4) identify the regular opportunities (annual customer meetings, inbound phone calls, a cry for help, etc.) to sell other products or services to customers.

Implementation

Clearly all this represents a significant amount of work. There's no escaping the fact. But you have to put the effort in if you are genuinely serious about growing your business.

Amongst all your other work commitments, you need to put aside one or two days a week (or more) to focus on growing the business. That's a lot of time for anyone – especially a partner of the business. But if you don't put this amount of effort in, we can assure you your targets won't be reached.

And in many cases that's where the problem lies. Most people are so busy working in the business that finding time to work ON the business is challenging to say the least.

Without doubt, managing your customer base as we have described will help free up more time. But you have to make a time commitment to growing the business. If you keep doing what you're doing, you're going to get what you've always got. So something has to change. You have to change and prioritize growing the business.

We recommend you block out your time to focus on growing the business. This means putting 'pretend' appointments in your calendar that you treat like real appointments.

Once you've done this you need to start tackling the actions we've highlighted. Systematically going through each action point is your best approach.

Only one person is going to change your business....YOU.

This is clearly true for a sole proprietor but is just as relevant for you if you are in a multiple partner business. It may be a slower process to turn around an oil tanker than a single-handed yacht, but in both cases the process starts by an individual turning the wheel. Leave it to someone else and you carry on as you are.

Black & Grey Widgets

Black & Grey have agreed that one of the partners will focus on growing the business. Everyone acknowledges that his task is going to be challenging and the meeting concludes with the statement, 'Just try and get done what you can'. It pleases the partner in charge of growing the business (John) because now he has a 'get out'. Nevertheless the meeting finishes on a high and everyone is looking forward to seeing the progress made over the next 6 months.

Rainbow Widgets

"As you can now see, growing a business isn't easy. There are dozens of things that need to be implemented. Dedicating time to creating, launching, testing and improving each element is especially time-consuming. But it is valuable work that has to be done.

"But as you know, there is a better way – a much better and easier way.

"The Business Growth System is one of the most successful marketing and business growth systems ever created. With step-by-step documents, templates and working examples all made even easier with video tutorials, you simply can't go wrong. Since you're a client of ours, what would ordinarily cost you over $5,000 to access, you can access for FREE. All you now need to do is appoint a partner responsible for the implementation of the system. It really is that simple."

14. Date Of Next Progress Meeting

Introduction

Both businesses, although they review progress at each monthly board meeting, agree to review the overall results in 6 months' time.

The partner responsible for the growth of each business will present the results. John will present for Black & Grey and Sarah will present for Rainbow Widgets.

14. Date Of Next Progress Meeting

Section 2: Progress Meeting

Results So Far

Introduction

The results of both businesses over a six-month period show a completely different picture. Where relevant, our comments are in the grey boxes. Take a look...

Black & Grey Widgets (By John)

<u>Summary Of Results</u>

- Inquiries Generated: 10 (6 by referral, 4 by general marketing).

> ### *<u>Our Comments...</u>*
>
> *This is a poor volume of inquiries for any business but typical of most businesses. Clearly it depends on what 'widget' you're selling in terms of the volume of inquiries you generate. If your widget is a machine costing tens of thousands of dollars, then your volume of inquiries will typically be lower than, say, a business selling widgets that cost far less. However, we can categorically state right now that whatever volume of inquiries you're getting at the moment – you can do better, much better by applying all the strategies in this book. If you're serious about growing your business, you should never be satisfied with your level of inquiries (how many can you generate when you're doing everything we recommend?).*

> *Clearly the level of inquiries you need is dependent on the number of customers you need to acquire to hit your acquisition targets for the next 12 months.*

- New Customers Acquired: 5 (4 through referral, 1 through general marketing).

Our Comments:

As you'd expect, the conversion of referral-based inquiries (66%) is significantly higher than general marketing inquiries (25%). Both these conversion rates are typical but are far too low for our liking.

You should be aiming for a conversion on referral inquiries of around 80-90% and 60-80% on general marketing inquiries. These results are achievable when you implement a sales conversion system.

- Customers Lost: 10 (6 moved to a competitor, 3 went bust, 1 sold).

Our Comments:

It's interesting that most businesses – even the good businesses – don't believe they have a customer attrition (customer losses) problem. Of course there's little you can do about natural attrition (people or businesses relocating, bankruptcies, etc.) but you should strive to have zero defections through unhappy customers.

Black & Grey, in the last six months, have started to see losses increase. Again this is typical. Most business owners and people in general have spent the last two years fire-fighting and as the economy slowly improves they are becoming more discerning and expecting much more from their suppliers.

> *You must deliver added value and exceptional service levels otherwise you too will suffer increasing customer losses, just as Black & Grey are experiencing.*

- Average Income From New Customers: $1,450 (per year).

Our Comments:

On its own, this figure is difficult to interpret; however, your overall objective with every customer is to increase their monetary value.

- Average Income Of Lost Customers: $1,900 (per year).

Our Comments:

Black & Grey have not only lost 10 customers – they've lost 10 good customers. It's interesting that when customers leave, they say 'your fees/prices are too high' but in reality this often means 'you're not providing enough value for money'.

Do NOT fall into the trap of thinking your fees or prices are too high – they rarely are. You should be thinking 'how can we add value to the relationships we have with our customers' and not 'how do we cut our prices'.

- Increase/Decrease In Average Prices/Fees Of Existing Customers: No change.

Our Comments:

The net loss in income from customer gains and customer losses is $11,750. This was tempered by the

> *strategy to increase prices 10% across all customers*
> *(a good one – but more effective if value had been*
> *added prior to the increase).*
>
> *Things are okay, but Black & Grey are barely*
> *holding their own. If you're standing still, in reality*
> *you're not – you're going backwards. Again, if you're*
> *looking to move your own business on, you cannot let*
> *it get into this position!*

Review

These first six months have been challenging on many fronts. The economy has obviously played a significant part in customer acquisitions and losses, but I have found it hard to implement a number of our initiatives due to a lack of time, not helped by having to fire-fight with existing customers.

I have been relatively pleased with the number of referrals we have had (6) that have converted into customers (4) although the number of new customers (1) through general marketing has not reached my expectations.

Referrals have increased because we started asking for them, although this has been a little bit 'hit or miss' since we find it awkward and difficult to ask for referrals.

Perhaps more disturbing is our number of customer losses (10) which, for only the second time in our history, have been more than customer gains (5). Plus, the majority of our losses are from long-term customers who have decided to change suppliers. This has resulted in an approximate overall loss of income of almost $12,000, although our 10% price increase has worked well (even though it may have contributed to some of the customer defections!) and means there is no overall net decrease in income (we have stayed roughly the same).

Elements Implemented

Market

- We agreed a target market of $2m - $5m.

> **_Our Comments:_**
>
> *This target market is challenging because it's a big jump from their 'bread-and-butter' customers. They don't have many other customers of the same type, so although targeting larger businesses is natural, it may take longer to convert them into customers.*
>
> *Notice only one new customer was gained from general marketing, which suggests two things: (1) the target market is challenging and (2) the marketing used was ineffective.*
>
> *This is a common occurrence, especially with the target market. As we said earlier, if you're not happy with the current size and scope of your customers, you cannot quickly move to much larger customers – you have to make small jumps in size. Yes it takes longer, but at least you will get there!*

Message

- Unique Perceived Benefit: Fixed Price Quotes.

> **_Our Comments:_**
>
> *Offering 'fixed price quotes' isn't unique. It's definitely something you should be offering (subject to obvious conditions), but it isn't going to make your target market sit up and think 'wow'.*

- Benefits: Proactive, personal service, value, reliability, support, service second to none.

> ### *Our Comments:*
>
> *None of these things are benefits – they are all features. Yet these terms and phrases are used extensively by 95% of businesses (in ALL industries).*
>
> *No one (and we repeat 'no one') gets excited by any of these things and you're deluding yourself if you think otherwise.*

- Irresistible Offer: Free no-obligation meeting.

> ### *Our Comments:*
>
> *Gary Halbert, the late, great copywriter, said you should imagine your prospect as a huge sloth of a man who's lying on his bed watching his favorite TV program.*
>
> *It's going to take a herculean effort for him to pick up the phone and request a meeting. Therefore your offer has to be so exciting, so different and so valuable to him that he actually drags himself away from his favorite TV program, and up from his bed to make the call.*
>
> *If your offer is like Black & Grey's, you've got problems.*

- Headline: Black & Grey.

> ### *Our Comments:*
>
> *We know you're proud of your business. We know it took a lot of blood, sweat and tears to get it to where it is today. But your customers and potential customers don't care about you. They care about*

> *what you can do for them. Your name as a headline is THE worst headline you could use.*

> *We have a good test for the quality of a headline. Imagine the headline is the entire ad. You can only add the words 'Call now for further information' after the headline. When you read the ad, it has to make you think, 'Yes I would call this business'.*

> *If it doesn't, then it's back to the drawing board. Obviously 'Black & Grey, call now for further information' doesn't pass this simple test!*

- Guarantee: None.

Our Comments:

Although guarantees are becoming more popular with a small number of businesses, they are still rarely used.

Remember, guarantees demonstrate to the customer that you stand behind your promises. They work very well at the point of purchase as a powerful sales conversion strategy and can also double up as a uniqueness in their own right. You omit them at your peril.

- Sales Barrier Demolition: None.

Our Comments:

The multi-stage guarantee has the capacity to transform your business overnight. Black & Grey, like so many businesses, don't appreciate the value of this little-known tactic.

> *Admittedly, sales barrier demolition is never easy to create, but once you've got something in place you will be astounded by its effectiveness.*

- Reasons Why: None.

Our Comments:

You don't need reasons why if you don't have an irresistible offer, a powerful guarantee or a sales barrier demolition strategy in place. Reasons why are necessary when your offer may sound sensational to the target market.

- Social Proof: Two testimonials.

Our Comments:

At least Black & Grey understand the value of using testimonials in their message. But, like everything we advise and recommend, there are right and wrong ways of doing it. Not putting the full name and the name of the business at the end of the testimonial is common – yet will immediately cast doubt over everything you say.

- Call To Action: None.

Our Comments:

Just putting a phone number at the end of your marketing piece doesn't constitute a call to action.

> *You have to build in something that reduces procrastination (stimulator) and summarize the offer.*

Media

- Direct Marketing Media, Published Media and E-Media.

> **Our Comments:**
>
> *This is good. Black & Grey are using all three media categories to reach the target market.*

Moment

- The same letter was mailed twice.

> **Our Comments:**
>
> *This is a very common approach to contacting the target market. In fact, Black & Grey have gone one better than most businesses in that at least they sent the letter out twice.*
>
> *Of course you can get lucky with this approach, whereby you 'catch' a few prospects at the right time, but by contacting the target market more frequently (at least once a month) the 'luckier' you'll get.*
>
> *This is a very basic phenomenon that is so easy to capitalize upon – yet so few do.*

Method

- Lead generation letter, business press advert and website.

> ## *Our Comments:*
>
> *Black & Grey correctly decided to use all three media categories; however, the website, letter and ad they used were all very typical. Very common. Very weak.*
>
> *None of them rise above the clutter. None of them have a complete message. None of them work anywhere near as well as they should (see example letter on next page).*

Black & Grey's Letter

B&G
Black & Grey
Widgets

Dear <Name>,

I am writing to introduce our firm to you. Black & Grey are an established firm of widget manufacturers.

Over the last ten years we have helped many businesses with our proactive and personal service. We are a business which prides itself on its close relationships with its customers and our service is second to none. Our approach to fixed price quotes is always popular and ensures you always know how much you will pay.

Here is what some of our clients have to say about us:

"I have used Black & Grey for over five years for all our widgets. Their professionalism and service has been exemplary. They adopt a 'can-do' attitude and are prepared to go the extra mile to satisfy a customer. I have no hesitation in recommending them to anyone seeking a widget manufacturer with a personal and professional service. Nice people to do business with!" - *AS - Stourbridge*

"Black & Grey provide a great selection of widgets. Their delivery and response times are always good and we always pay what they quote us." - *PN - Gloucester*

We offer a full range of widgets and support services including maintenance contracts, servicing packages and consulting at very competitive prices.

We would like to take this opportunity to meet with you. We offer a free no-obligation meeting. Simply call us at **0123 456 789** and we'll be happy to discuss how we can help with your widget needs.

Why Businesses Stop Growing...

If you would like any further information, please do not hesitate to contact us on the number below.

Yours sincerely,

For and on behalf of Black & Grey

Black & Grey Widgets
Any Street, Any Town, Any City, Any Postcode
Tel: 0123 456 7890 Fax: 0123 456 7891
Web: blackandgreywidgets.co.uk

Actions – The 4 Practice Multipliers

More Inquiries By Referral

- Partners and sales staff were tasked with asking customers for referrals.

Our Comments:

This is not a system. In most businesses, partners and staff – even sales staff – are reluctant to ask for referrals as they find it awkward and even embarrassing. Therefore results will at best be hit or miss.

You need to put something in place that takes away this awkwardness and also ensures a high take-up rate from customers.

More Inquiries By General Marketing

- The website was already in place. A display ad for the business press was created and placed, and a one-page lead generation letter was created.

Our Comments:

> *Black & Grey have restricted their growth by NOT using more marketing strategies across each media category.*
>
> *Your aim should be to have at least a dozen marketing strategies spread across the media categories. If every one of these strategies was working well for you, just think about what that would mean to your business.*

Converting More Inquiries Into Sales (Sales Conversion)

- No changes were implemented here.

> ### Our Comments:
>
> *Black & Grey's conversion rates are not industry-leading. They are very typical, but could be so much better. The combination of having a sales conversion system in place alongside a unique competitive advantage, and a host of other strategies we have highlighted throughout this book, would transform conversion rates.*
>
> *Remember, improving the conversion of inquiries into customers doesn't cost a single penny!*

Maximizing Prices/Fees From Customers

- The 10% overall increase in prices was executed and helped to steady the ship as customer losses exceeded customer gains.

> ### Our Comments:

> *Black & Grey's strategy of a 10% increase across all customers was a wise move and demonstrates that most businesses don't charge enough.*
>
> *However, without adding value to the relationship they have with customers, this is a dangerous ploy and may be responsible for a number of customer losses.*

Rainbow Widgets

Summary Of Results

- Inquiries Generated: 38 (22 by referral, 16 by general marketing).

> *Our Comments...*
>
> *This is more like it! If you're looking to grow, you have to accept that generating inquiries is the lifeblood of your business.*
>
> *You have to be prolific in this area if you want to dominate your competition.*

- New Customers Acquired: 27 (17 through referral, 10 through general marketing).

> *Our Comments:*
>
> *Conversion of referrals is approaching 80% and conversion of general marketing is just over 60%.*

> *Both these results are getting close to industry-best figures, but there is still room for improvement.*

- Customers Lost: 6 (2 moved to another supplier, 3 went bust, 1 retired).

Our Comments:

There is nothing you can do about four of the six customers lost (natural attrition). But losing just two customers is a good result in this economic climate. Nevertheless the business should work hard to try and reduce these to zero.

- Average Income From New Customers: $2,350 (per year).

Our Comments:

Notice the difference here compared to Black & Grey. Almost $1,000 more per year per customer.

- Average Income Of Lost Customers: $1,900 (per year).

Our Comments:

These were also two good customers lost, but notice that new customers are generating more sales income!

- Increase/Decrease In Average Prices Of Existing Customers: 12% increase.

Our Comments:

> *This is a great result. A 12% increase on top of the increase in overall prices through new customer acquisition is a significant step forward.*

Review

We are a good business, but as we all agreed, we needed to do something different if we wanted to see a better result than our previous 12 months.

I have to say the first 6 months' results have shown how successful it can be to put a marketing system in place.

We appointed Rachel to implement the system. She spends a day a week on the system and I oversee it.

The whole process has really opened my eyes to what we can achieve as a business. We have, through the years, all been frustrated in the knowledge that we deserve to be doing better, and now we have the solution. I wish we'd done this years ago.

I would also say that in the early months we were a little worried about the style of the marketing. In fact, we held back on a few things but once we saw results in other areas, we just put these thoughts behind us and now we just do it.

So, in summary, we have acquired 27 new customers. 17 through referral and 10 through general marketing. These new customers have an anticipated average income of $2,350 which is well above our existing customer average income.

Customer losses are also down. We lost 6 in the period but only 2 left to competitors. Again we should be pleased with this.

Probably the best news is that we have increased prices by 12% and new customer acquisitions have increased sales and revenue by another $60,000.

Elements Implemented

Market

- After carefully analyzing our customer base, we decided to target mid-range businesses with revenue of $400k - $1m. Most of our sales and profits come from businesses with revenue of $200k - $750k, but we wanted to target slightly larger customers.

Our Comments:

The target market choice is sensible. Yes they decided to target slightly larger businesses, but the jump in size is relatively small. Small enough not to matter to any potential new customer. Their results reinforce that the target market choice has been successful.

Message

- Unique Perceived Benefit: 24-hour delivery or the order is free.

> ### *Our Comments:*
>
> *Speed, as we mentioned earlier in the book, is a great way of creating uniqueness. Since none of the competition is offering delivery in less than 24 hours, this is a powerful message to the target market. Key to such a strategy is ensuring you can 'deliver' on the promise. Do not ever promise something you can't deliver on 95% of the time.*

- Benefits: Many.

> ### *Our Comments:*
>
> *It's surprising to many how easy it is to transform features into benefits. Remember, we advocate using both features and benefits as they form a potent combination.*

- Irresistible Offer: Free no-obligation meeting with clear reasons why the meeting is worthwhile and a free special report titled 'The 6 Common Mistakes Most Businesses Make When Buying Widgets'.

> ### *Our Comments:*
>
> *The special report reinforces your expertise and is highly desirable to people who are about to buy the 'widget'. The meeting is described in detail, in terms of the benefits it will bring to the prospective customer. Just because you offer something for free doesn't mean people will automatically go for it. You*

> *have to 'sell' it – and sell it hard. If people can genuinely see that giving*
>
> *up their time is more than worth it – they'll be more compelled to meet with you.*
>
> *All in all, getting meetings with the target market is made much easier with this approach.*

- Headline: Many tested. Here's the one which is currently working best: "Guaranteed Overnight Delivery Of Widgets – Or Your Whole Order Is Free".

> **_Our Comments:_**
>
> *You cannot underestimate the difference good headlines will have on your entire sales and marketing system. Use them in EVERY marketing piece you ever create.*

- Guarantee: The UPB is of course a guarantee, but this is supported with the following:

> 'All our widgets come with a 100% money-back guarantee. If within the first 60 days you are at all unhappy with the widget, just send it back to us and we'll refund every single penny, no questions asked.'

> **_Our Comments:_**
>
> *A guarantee like this reverses the risk and reduces the barriers to sale. If you have a good widget then guaranteeing its quality in this way will instantly increase sales. Plus a welcome by-product of a guarantee like this adds considerable value to your promise. Compare something like this to a competitor who doesn't offer a guarantee! Who would you choose to do business with?*

- Sales Barrier Demolition: The UPB and the guarantee in this instance are so powerful that a sales barrier demolition isn't required. However, the following was also added...

  'All widgets are made to the highest standards. If within 5 years they stop working (other than from normal wear and tear) we'll replace them completely free of charge.'

> ### *Our Comments:*
>
> *Sometimes the power of your UPB and guarantee eliminates the need for a sales barrier demolition. But even if this is the case, look to see if there are other important elements of your widget that you can further guarantee. The more risk you're prepared to take, the greater your sales. Simple.*

- Reasons Why: Here it is...

  'So why do we offer this guarantee? Simple really. Last year we sold 3,248 widgets. In every case we delivered them on time – every time. But we know how important speed of delivery is to you. Therefore, to put your mind at rest, we guarantee next-day delivery. And if we mess up – we suffer, not you. Isn't that how it should be?'

> ### *Our Comments:*
>
> *Do not underestimate the importance of reasons why. As you can see in this example, the reasons why act to justify the offer **and** reinforce the importance of why you're doing it. It makes for compelling reading.*

- Social Proof: A number of testimonials.

> ### *Our Comments:*

> *For something so simple, it still amazes us how few businesses use testimonials in their marketing. Put it this way: more testimonials = more sales!*

- Call To Action: Here it is...

  'To arrange your free no-obligation meeting, simply call us at 0987 654 321 or e-mail us at support@rainbowwidgets.com. Remember, during the meeting we'll explain the 6 common mistakes most businesses make when buying widgets. And whether you decide to buy or not, we'll leave our special report with you. As an added incentive, if you arrange your meeting within the next 14 days, we'll knock 10% off your first order, should you decide to buy. Thank you.'

> **_Our Comments:_**
>
> *Clearly this is a very general call to action because of the nature of this book, but even in this context you should be able to see why this is such a powerful way to ensure people don't procrastinate and ultimately make that all-important call (or e-mail)!*

Media

- Direct Marketing Media, Published Media and E-Media.

> **_Our Comments:_**
>
> *As we mentioned earlier, the key is to have multiple strategies working tirelessly for you in each media. The more – the better.*

Moment

Why Businesses Stop Growing...

- The target market was contacted 6 times (once a month).

> ## *Our Comments:*
>
> *The more you contact your target market – the greater the response. However, your marketing pieces must rise above the clutter to get noticed – otherwise your efforts will be wasted.*

Method

- Innovative postcards (x4), website landing page, Yellow Pages ad, referral system for customers, press releases, Google AdWords, past customer reactivation letter, letter to past prospects, monthly newsletter.

  On the following pages you can see a number of examples of the types of marketing pieces that you can use to rise above the clutter.

> ## *Our Comments:*
>
> *As you can see, Rainbow Widgets have been very active. Whether you like it or not – you have to be prolific in getting your message out to your target market. You don't have to do it all at once. Just make sure you add marketing strategies to each media each month and build it gradually. Even if all you do is add 2 per month, within 6 months you'll have 12 strategies all contributing to your growth.*

Why Businesses Stop Growing...

Marketing Pieces That Get Noticed

<u>Invitations</u>

Invitations are virtually impossible to ignore. They don't need to be elaborate like the one shown here, but make sure your outer envelope includes the words 'Invitation enclosed. RSVP'.

Why Businesses Stop Growing...

<u>Comics</u>

Comics get very high readership.
This is the front page of a 4-page comic.

Postcards

Postcards have one advantage over all other forms of direct mail – they're already 'open'. They are a cost-effective way to get your message to your target market.

'Tear Sheets'

Tear Sheets are simulated articles written by a fictitious third party promoting your product or service. Notice the Post-It note on the top right.

<u>X-Ray</u>

We defy anyone not to open this! The 'x-ray' image inside should have a headline like... "Is <Biggest Problem You Solve> Giving You A Headache?"

Why Businesses Stop Growing...

Newsletters

Tech-Ni-Tips
Feb 2008

World Class Print Finishing Advice & Product Updates

Inside This Issue

- Product News & Update
- Customer Feedback
- Graham's Tip Of the Month
- Special Offer
- Ordering Information

Product Range:

Tri-creaser (attaches to the following folding machines to completely eliminate fibre-cracking)

- Stahl/Heidelberg
- MBO
- Herzog & Heymann
- GUK
- Horizon
- Shoei
- Bremmer
- Morgana
- MB
- Eurofold
- Rollem
- Baum
- Rosback

Spine Creaser (attaches to the following Stitching machines to eliminate fibre-cracking on all your book covers)

- Muller Martini
- Heidelberg ST-100, ST-300

Micro-Perf (attaches to the following folding machines resulting in perfect perforations, even on paper)

- Stahl
- Heidelberg
- MBO

Accessories

Please call for details

How To Order

Please phone our Order Hotline at 0116 275 1440

Product Update And Latest News

Tech-ni-fold USA Launched…

I am delighted to inform you that our USA agents (CRN) have signed a contract to distribute our products under the Tech-ni-fold banner. Tech-ni-fold USA will continue to implement our proven sales and marketing strategies and at the same time help us to expand our product range throughout the US. The agreement enforces a total commitment to Tech-ni-fold products.

Sales in this initial first year have already led to us almost doubling up the manufacturing of our products with a significant growth continuing month by month.

DRUPA 2008…Two Stands Secured…

I am very excited by the news that we have taken a large stand at DRUPA in May.

This fantastic opportunity was secured through our association with Stielow, the Horizon re-sellers based in Germany who ran across us at IPEX two years ago.

The stand will be taken up by Tech-ni-fold USA and compliment our own activities from the British PICON area in Hall 10 (10E66-2)

Advertising Opportunity

If you are finding that our products are making a significant difference to your company, we would like to hear from you.

In return for your much valued statements and a good picture of people next to machines etc. we will add a small company summary and contact details if required. If chosen your company will also receive a free Tri-creaser upgrade.

We plan to run a full colour page advert in the PrintWeek magazine, read by over 20,000 people. We are also seeking testimonials from our customers and are offering 5 FREE creasing inserts for every faxed statement explaining the benefits of any of our products. Constructive criticism and feedback is always welcome as we can make use of this to move forward.

Page 1 of 2 - please turn over...

Graham's Tip Of the Month

How To Perfectly Match The Creasing Rib Into Channel During Make-Ready (Tri-creaser)

In case you find it difficult to centralise one of the female channels against the male Creasing rib, here is a simple way to guarantee 100% perfect alignment.

Secure the Tri-creaser Male component into the correct crease position. Move female part directly opposite without securing the fixing grub screw.

Wind some heavy stock backwards passing through the device, towards the fixing rollers. Secure the fixing grub screw on female part with Allen key when it appears.

Now you will witness the perfect alignment.

How To Feed Sheets With Aperture Or Window Cut Outs

Feeding a flat sheet with apertures or window cut outs can prove to be impossible, as the top sheet will catch on the one below as it leaves the feeder.

In order to simplify the explanation on how to avoid this I will describe the remedy for a pile feeder (not continuous).

Continued overleaf...

Newsletters are one of the most undervalued marketing strategies available to any business. Fill them with quality content and stuff that's interesting (it doesn't all have to be relevant to your industry).

Actions – The 4 Practice Multipliers

More Inquiries By Referral

- The 'Customer Referral System' was activated.

> ***Our Comments:***
>
> *A customer referral system is one of the easiest and lucrative things you can implement. There simply isn't any excuse for not having one!*

More Inquiries By General Marketing

- Innovative postcards (x4), website landing page, Yellow Pages ad, referral system for customers, press releases, Google AdWords, past customer reactivation letter, letter to past prospects, monthly newsletter.

> ***Our Comments:***
>
> *There are many more general marketing activities that could have been implemented over the 6-month period, but the key to all this is to implement something EVERY month.*

Converting More Inquiries Into Sales (Sales Conversion)

- The Sales Conversion System was implemented.

> ***Our Comments:***
>
> *No matter what industry you're in, a sales conversion system will make a huge difference to*

> *your sales. Remember it costs you virtually nothing to implement and the results are instant!*

Maximizing Prices/Fees From Customers

- The 12% increase was achieved by reducing customer losses, adding value, up-selling and cross-selling and using the newsletter to give customers special offers.

> ### Our Comments:
>
> *As we said earlier, getting customers to buy more and to buy more frequently is without doubt the easiest way to grow any business. Key leverage points are selling more at the point of purchase (using up-sell and cross-sell) and using a monthly newsletter with customer special offers.*

Summary

That concludes this second section of the book. Hopefully you can see that implementing a marketing system in your business can often transform it overnight.

The key is to implement the key stages we've taken you through.

But we're now only two-thirds of the way to creating the perfect business. Next, you need to take a firm grip on the management of the business. That leads us on to Section 3...

15. Management Function: Introduction

In the first section of this book we explained why the growth and development of many businesses gets stifled. Businesses that were once dynamic and progressive become victims of their growth because it is a growth driven by process. The emphasis is on what a business does and not on the actual running of the business. As a result, the business gets busier but not more productive. It generates more sales, at least until it plateaus, but profits don't grow proportionately. What do grow are the levels of frustration and stress and the number of problems.

Let's go back to the three components in business model.

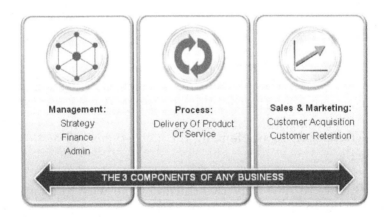

Management:
Strategy
Finance
Admin

Process:
Delivery Of Product
Or Service

Sales & Marketing:
Customer Acquisition
Customer Retention

THE 3 COMPONENTS OF ANY BUSINESS

With the emphasis on process, a business can grow in the short and medium term simply by doing a good job for its customers. The service is top quality and very personal. Customers, happy with the work, come back for more and recommend others. Eventually the business starts to enter a

cycle of getting busier and busier. Less time and more pressure sees a
falling-off of service and an increase in customer complaints. With less time for running and marketing the business, the problems multiply and the good days become a thing of the past.

We've written about the need to take back control of your business by bringing the focus back on to its management and marketing. In Section 2 we then showed you how to create sales and marketing systems that put you back in control and produce results without taking you away from your process. We introduced you to the strategies that generate four vital components of business growth: more of the right inquiries, more conversions into customers, better customer retention and maximizing the financial value of your customers.

The result is not only more customers and more sales but more cash and more profit. Is it the perfect business, though?

A business that's excellent at what it does and markets itself effectively is clearly a business with the potential for success. Yet we've not yet solved the issue of being too busy. We're profitable but not as profitable as we should be. We have more cash coming in but cash flow can still be a problem.

One of the dangers businesses face as they turn the corner, especially in periods of wider economic downturn such as we face now, is the risk of so-called 'overtrading'. Customer activity picks up and this places demands on workloads, consumables and stock levels. If the business isn't managed effectively, then the increased sales simply result in greater inefficiencies, higher costs and more demands on cash. In other words, an increase in sales can lead to less cash and less profit.

Time, therefore, to bring our focus on to the last of our three components: management.

Why Businesses Stop Growing...

The next page shows the 4 key components of management and how they combine to give you a very successful business...

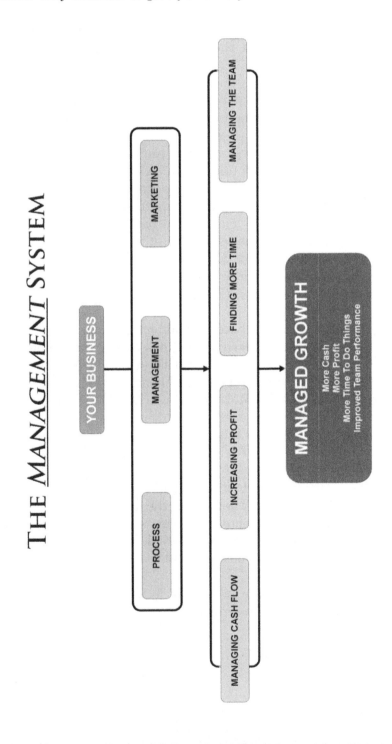

Let's now return to our two businesses, Black and Grey Widgets and Rainbow Widgets. The partners of Black and Grey have continued doing things the way they always have.

Not only is the business struggling to show any real growth but the frustrations and problems that they face through lack of performance don't seem to be getting any less. Week after week the business grinds on. It's okay, but it's a million miles from what they had dreamed about and looks like staying that way far into the future. Still, fingers crossed that something will come along.

The partners at Rainbow Widgets are seeing a different picture. Having followed the strategies outlined earlier in this book, business is booming.

The systems that they've put in place are generating high-quality new business but in a very timely and cost-effective manner that has actually reduced the amount of time and money that they put into their marketing. Removing the unwanted customers had helped them to free up further time and resources and the business was starting to benefit from a significantly enhanced reputation and profile. The job's not done yet, though. While the process and sales and marketing functions are working extremely well, the management of the business needs to be significantly improved if they are to see the full benefits of the changes they've made.

It's coming up to monthly board meeting time again and both sets of partners are settling down to address their issues. Let's join them...

Why Businesses Stop Growing...

16. Why Do We Keep Running Out Of Cash?

Introduction

To some business managers, cash is the only measure they have of their business performance. Whether or not they have available funds in the bank determines their assessment of the state of play that day. It's a dangerous and wholly inaccurate means of measurement, simply because the amount of cash in your business is both a symptom and a result, an outcome of many different influences and actions going on within the business.

Here are some of the more common reasons why a business finds itself facing cash flow pressures:

- Lack of investment for the size and type of business

- Expenditure exceeds income

- Poor use of funding options, in particular spending short-term funds on long-term assets

- Poor credit control

- Slow invoicing procedures

- Ineffective terms and conditions with customers

- Weak supplier management

- Staff under-performance

Why Businesses Stop Growing...

- Poor production control

- Excessive owner drawings

- Bad debts

- Changes to funding arrangements

- Downturn in the market

- Sudden upturn in the market

- Loss-making or weak profit margins

- Theft

- Unforeseen costs

- Unplanned production delays

- Over-stocking

- Errors in costing

- Significant swings in business levels

The list could go on and on. Take a look at the list and ask yourself this question: "Could any negative impact of this factor on the cash flow of the business be reduced or removed if management was more aware and more in control in this particular area?"

The simple answer is surely "Yes". In many cases, the problem is completely eradicated by better management. In all cases, its impact is lessened by a management team that is aware, focused and in control.

Let's start at the beginning...

1. How much money does your business need?

It's too late to start your business again. We can't go back and look at what funding ideally should have been in place on Day 1 but we can look at what is going to be needed from now.

Every day you're faced with making financial decisions within your business.

"I need to buy some equipment. Can I afford it?"

"I've got a supplier on the phone demanding payment. What do I say?"

"My staff are due a pay raise. How much should I give them?"

"I've got money in the bank at last. Is it safe for me to have a bonus?"

If you don't know what your cash requirements are, how can you plan for them and manage them? Quite simply, you can't.

Every decision you take and action you apply has an effect on the finances and cash flow of your business down the line. Every decision directly or indirectly affects every subsequent one. If you don't understand the impact of your decisions on the future of your business, then each action becomes a lottery. Businesses frequently run out of cash because of decisions that have previously been made without the full implications being known.

So you have to start by creating your financial plan: your forecast for how you expect the business to move in financial terms.

Why Businesses Stop Growing...

For some, this is seen as a theoretical exercise and a chore to be carried out only if your banker asks for it. This is missing the point. Before you go on vacation, you estimate how much money you're going to need. Even when getting ready for a night out, most people check their wallet or purse and quickly determine if they have enough cash. And yet business managers regularly start and run their businesses with no proper consideration of how much money they are going to need, and indeed, whether they are going to have enough.

Business decisions are made on the basis of, "Yeah, it'll be okay". Consequently, businesses run out of money because the manager hasn't taken the time and trouble to look ahead. The business hits a brick wall that should have been easily spotted.

Creating a financial forecast is easy. First, you need to understand what your objective is for creating the forecast. Is this a long-term plan to help you ascertain the level of investment in the business? If so, this could warrant you preparing figures for the next three or five years, or even longer. Possibly it is a plan to look at your business decisions over the next 12 months, a picture of the year ahead. It could even be a survival plan, showing which bills you can pay over the next four weeks.

As a rule of thumb, the longer the plan, the more strategic it becomes and the less detail it requires. It becomes a summary of the years ahead. The more immediate the forecast, the more detail it requires, getting down to individual transactions in the case of a survival plan for the next few days and weeks.

Once you understand what you are trying to learn from the forecast and what period and level of detail is appropriate, then you can create your forecast. Most managers will use one of a range of available forecasting software packages to help do this, or create their own on their computers' existing spreadsheet software.

Keep the construction as simple as possible. The forecast needs to be accurate but easy to follow and not so complicated that you can't see the forest through the trees. Ask yourself:

What income do I expect to come in and when?

What costs do I have to pay and when?

Break both down into weeks, months or years depending on the time period you are working to.

It's that easy.

Once you understand your cash inflows and outflows and the expected peaks and troughs, then you are in a much better position to make financial decisions and to take action to counter opportunities and threats identified in the future.

You cannot successfully run a business without this tool. Any other way is a lottery. Go back to the list of common reasons why businesses face cash-flow pressures. Do you see now why having updated financial forecasts in place helps to avoid and address many of these?

2. Getting the cash in

This isn't going to be an issue for cash-based transactions and typical business-to-consumer establishments where credit isn't offered, but let's consider the millions of transactions made each year where a receivable can potentially be created at the point of sale.

You've done the difficult bit. You've captured the interest of your customer, converted them into getting an order, met the order and delivered the goods. Where's your money?

Let's put it another way...

You've spent money on marketing to attract the interest of the customer. You've spent time and money converting them from a potential customer to an actual one. You've incurred considerable cost in stock, labor, equipment and overheads in order to produce the order. You've possibly incurred delivery costs. In other words, until the customer actually pays you, your bank account faces a heavy loss.

That's one customer. Now multiply that by the number of customers who owe you money for goods and services not yet paid for. Now are you starting to get an idea of where your money has gone?

For many businesses there is a time gap between incurring the true costs of producing their goods or services and the customer actually paying for them. The business funds the cost of this time gap, usually via its bank line of credit. In busier times this funding gap can get even bigger as more and more orders are met and costs and accounts receivable rise. So going out and chasing more orders can accentuate the cash-flow problem.

Credit control is typically seen as chasing outstanding accounts receivable. A vital function and one that is badly done in too many businesses. But let's look beyond the invoice.

The cash deficit starts from the first point of contact with a customer – the inquiry and subsequent conversion into a customer. At this point, you have already started spending money on this customer through your marketing budget. This is the point, therefore, from which you start to manage your credit control.

You do this by ensuring that they become a customer on your terms. Your marketing will already have laid out to the customer the benefits of their using your company. You now need to make it quite clear to them what you are looking to get out of the relationship. There's nothing wrong with explaining to a new customer how you intend to make a profit and get paid, and most importantly, what their responsibilities are in this respect.

If the business relationship is to be successful, then it has to work to the benefit of both parties. A customer who doesn't appreciate this is a customer you don't want.

The formalizing of this comes within your terms and conditions. Let's be quite clear on this point... Every customer should be handed a copy of your terms and conditions before they do business with you, and acknowledge their acceptance of them. These should be clear, concise, simple and meaningful. The terms and conditions form an integral part of your armory and armor for any subsequent dispute, so they are absolutely vital. Terms & Conditions are not a thing to be simply copied from the back of another company's invoice. They should be an accurate record of the basis of business between you and your customer. **You risk everything by failing to put them properly in place.**

Your customer has now been properly signed up with a clear understanding of what you expect from them. They proceed to place an order with you. Here's the next stage of your credit control, and we're still a long way from issuing an invoice in many businesses. At this point you need to ensure that you and the customer have the same understanding and expectations. You should create an order confirmation, detailing the nature of the order, any obligations of the customer and you, the timetable, the price and the payment details. A good test is to ask yourself, "What could go wrong on this job?" and ensure that your order confirmation properly protects your back by positioning the expectations and understanding of the customer alongside your own.

Up to this point, you have successfully minimized the potential for dispute and argument and strengthened your hand should one still arise. Now you can move on with the order. This too has cash-flow implications, but more of that later.

Your order is completed and the goods and services supplied to the customer. Make sure now that you obtain a receipt from the customer. "Yes, I have received what I ordered and it is what I expected and requested"...or not. Any dispute is now quickly resolved, backed up by the T & Cs and order confirmation you already have in place.

Now invoice the customer without further delay. It's amazing just how many businesses wait until the end of the week, or month, or even longer, before billing. There is no reason to, other than a lack of discipline within the business. Think how many invoices you issue during the course of your working year. Let's say it's 50 per month. Now let's assume that you bill monthly. Assuming you complete your work evenly through the month, that means on average you complete roughly 12 jobs per week. The delay to invoicing is therefore:

- 12 jobs delayed by approximately 3 weeks
- 12 jobs delayed by approximately 2 weeks
- 12 jobs delayed by approximately 1 week

The rest are billed promptly. 6 weeks, that's 30 days in total during which customers have had no opportunity to pay you because they've not seen an invoice despite receiving the goods or service. Over a year, that's a total of 360 days that customers of the business have been in possession of the goods without an invoice.

The next stage is just as important. Should you offer your customers credit, and if so, how long should it be? You don't have to offer credit in any industry. Forget what your competitors are doing or what is the industry 'norm' here. Make your own decision. Let's consider what really matters...

You have to be customer-friendly and therefore making it as easy as possible for customers to afford your products and pay for your products is very important. However, credit grew in a time when customers didn't have all the payment options that they have now. Credit cards, debit cards, PayPal, credit agreements, finance loans, the list goes on. Consider carefully, therefore, whether it is actually necessary for you to be the one taking the credit risk or whether you can achieve a similar customer-friendly approach by offering different options that get your money in sooner. Offering guarantees (discussed earlier in this book) is a proven method you can use to minimize the risk of buying from you, and therefore because this risk is low – you can quite easily demand payment upfront from your customers.

Assuming credit remains on your list of options, the next point to consider is who are you going to offer credit to. It certainly doesn't need to be, and possibly shouldn't be, everyone. Should new customers get it automatically? Probably not. Should customers with a poor payment history continue to receive it? Definitely not. Credit is there to be earned. It isn't a right.

There are a variety of ways of assessing the credit worthiness of new customers. Credit-scoring agencies abound online. You can seek business references. You can adopt your own system based on the production of key data from the customer. All have their benefits and downside. Ultimately, it comes down to how much you want the business and how much of a risk you are prepared to take.

Existing poor payers should know that they face the risk of losing the benefit. Anyone who doesn't abide by your terms and conditions should face a potential penalty, or what's the point of having them?

The important thing is that you take a moment to consider their creditworthiness and make an assessment. Actively decide whether this customer and this transaction has earned the right to credit with your firm. If not, don't give it.

For those customers who have earned the right to credit terms, you must also consider the period of credit. One month, or 30 days, tends to be offered without much thought. Again, let's ignore what others do and look at your own circumstances.

The credit you offer should take into account the timing of your cash outflows linked to the sale. If your staff is paid monthly, then 30 days' credit may be appropriate, but is this still the case if your staff is paid weekly? Look at your suppliers. If you offer credit terms to your customers more favorable than the ones you receive from your suppliers, then you are always going to be out of pocket.

Let's say that you buy and sell widgets. You get 7 days' credit from your supplier and give your customer 30 days. You pay your supplier before you're paid yourself and are out of pocket for another three weeks at least. Too few businesses consider this aspect of their cash flow and yet it is an opportunity to get ahead of the game.

Now we can move on to the area that most people would consider to be credit control. You've created your invoice, given your credit and are now waiting to get paid. What do you do?

Like every other aspect of your business, you should create a system internally that means that you manage and control the process rather than leaving it in the hands of others.

If you want to be paid on time, then having a system in place that reminds customers of upcoming liabilities and offers them incentives for settlement is crucial.

How about an e-mail to your customer one week before the invoice is due:

Save $62.35 Now

"Just a polite reminder that invoice no. 2334, totaling $1,247.15, is due for payment by January 28th 2013. We offer a discount of 5% for all invoices paid within the agreed terms.

You can therefore save **$62.35** if you pay this invoice within the next 7 days.

"If, for whatever reason, you will not be able to make payment by January 28th, please contact us now."

You would include in your e-mail details of the various ways in which the customer can pay you.

Early payment discounts can easily be factored into your initial costings, and in any case, are a more cost-effective solution for your business than the time and money incurred in debt collection.

Some managers find that concerns over damaging the customer relationship get in the way of effective credit control. Early payment discounts are a much more positive solution than charging interest on overdue accounts, and so can help in this respect. The end result is the same.

Let's say that the price of your product is $50. You know that you intend to offer a discount of 5% for early payment. The price of your goods is therefore uplifted to $52.63 ($50/95 x 100) with discount available of $2.63. Good payers, paying on time and taking the discount, therefore pay the 'true' price of $50. Bad payers effectively end up paying a $2.63 penalty.

Of course, the percentage you apply is entirely up to you.

"But what happens if someone takes the discount but still pays late?" we hear some of you cry. Like everything else in your business, you can take a view depending on who it is. In a genuine case you may let them off, perhaps with a friendly reminder. For those abusing the system, the debt still applies and you decide on their eligibility for ongoing credit.

Hopefully, all your customers have now paid their bills on time. We all know that's not going to happen! Now we get on with the process of chasing overdue accounts.

You can be completely bullish about this. There's nothing to stop you taking immediate steps for debt collection via the courts or an agency the moment a debt breaches your terms and conditions. Word would quickly get around that you are not to be messed with, and in a world where cash is limited for many businesses, you would push yourself to the top of most payment lists. It's a valid strategy. It's maybe not the best for ongoing customer relationships but you can argue that a business doesn't want or need slow payers.

You need to ensure that your terms and conditions, and your paperwork in general, are all up to this approach but if you are comfortable with such a clear-cut approach, then we're certainly not going to try to dissuade you. It's simple, effective and everyone knows where they stand.

For many, this approach would be seen as a little too aggressive. There are, of course, many reasons why customers don't pay on time. Some we have sympathy with, others deserve little support. It's fair to say that the majority of business managers prefer to have some flexibility in their approach to allow them to manage individual customers' circumstances. The challenge is to do this without weakening your own cash flow and allowing others to dictate the relationship.

The key is the quality and systematic nature of your communication with the debtor. You have to start managing the situation as soon as the debt becomes overdue, and that means talking to them - firmly, regularly and often.

You have a decision to make very early on... is this a genuine case for support (in which case, do you want to/can you afford to support?) or is this someone testing out your weakness, using you to fund their business?

Let's not forget that the debtor has ordered and received goods or services from you. How were they intending to pay you when they placed their order? It's a fair question.

Through your consideration of a customer's entitlement to credit, you have already reduced the chances of payment delay at this stage, but if this is a case of deliberately not paying, your previous good preparation will now really come to the forefront. If you have followed the process, then you have your case lined up already.

- Clear terms and conditions that they have accepted and are now in breach of.

- A confirmed order from the customer, accepting your price and your understanding of their requirements.

- A signed delivery receipt with proof of delivery and acceptance.

The customer's grounds for dispute have been systematically removed by your process. In most cases, therefore, this now simply becomes a matter for debt collection. Pass it over to your lawyer or debt-collection service without delay or take action yourself through the small-claims procedure.

Do no further work for this type of customer.

We live in a reasonable world full of reasonable people. The likelihood is that, for most overdue debtors, they thought that they would be able to pay you when they ordered the goods or service, and certainly intend to pay you, but through poor cash management of their own, or change of circumstance, they find themselves unable to meet the full debt on the due day.

You decide that this is a genuine case. The first consideration, therefore, is: are you willing to support them?

Essentially, do you want to continue your relationship with this customer? If the answer is "No", then it's straight to your formal debt-collection procedure.

If you are willing to support, then your next question has to be: "Can I afford to?" If you are in a bigger financial mess than they are, then you have to protect your own position. Like it or not, you have to get tough with them and apply your debt-collection procedure.

If you are willing and able to support a genuine case, then you have to manage the process. You could be cash-rich and a generous benefactor. You could simply say, "Hey, don't worry about it. Pay me when you can. Now, what's your next order?"

It would be good to be in that position but most aren't, and arguably, those who are won't stay in that position for long if this is their approach. You can be firm and fair in your support.

The key is regular and clear communication. The moment you are aware of an overdue account, you should call them and find out what the problem is and what their plans are to address it.

If they can't afford to pay the whole debt now, find out how much they can afford to pay you and when you will receive it. Agree when you are going to call them again to get the next installment. Regular contact with continuous progress in reducing the debt is what you are looking for.

You have to maintain this, though. If they are under cash pressure, then it won't be just you who is chasing them for money. The customer will be working with limited funds and having to prioritize these on a weekly basis. You can't allow yourself to be pushed off the payment list each week.

By being fair but firm, you can maintain regular money coming in, but of course, they have to be fair to you in return. Whether by choice or not, they cannot use you to fund their business. If they won't or can't work with you to reduce the debt, then you have to step up the pressure. If that means resorting eventually to debt collection, then so be it, but the customer can avoid this by working with you to get the debt down.

Reducing the debt means just that. Too many businesses make the mistake of allowing their exposure to bad debt to increase by continuing to provide goods and services for customers with overdue debts. If you produce new work for a customer quicker than they are paying off old debt, then your exposure and risk can only increase... and quickly, if you're not careful.

By all means, continue to work for customers who you are supporting on the credit management side, but do this in a managed fashion as well. If the customer is paying off old debt at $500 per week, for example, make sure that new work is restricted to a lower figure to allow the overall exposure to credit to reduce, so that new work is paid on delivery.

As with every other aspect of your business, the trick is to ensure that you manage the process and not let circumstances manage you.

Good credit control is a process with each stage adding to the strength of your cash flow (see next page).

The Full Cycle Credit Control Plan

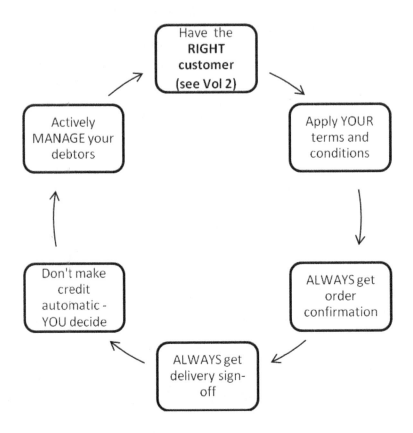

3. Speeding up the process

We asked at the start of this section, "Where does all the money go?" Here's a great exercise to do in your business. Think about what happens from the moment a customer places an order. It doesn't matter what your business does. In general terms, it's something like this:

- **Preparation Stage**
  Planning
  Allocation of resources

- **Production Stage**

Process
Creation

- **Delivery Stage**
  Sign-off
  Customer hand-over

Identify each stage in your business. Think how long each stage takes you. Now think about what cash goes out of your business at that stage...wages, materials, overheads, etc.

Each one of these stages costs your business time and money. The longer the duration of the stage, the greater the cash outlay.

Now ask yourself... "Does work pass through each stage as quickly and efficiently as it possibly could?"

Probably not.

The amount of cash that you have in your business is directly affected by how efficient you are at getting your goods and services into the hands of your customer.

In the following chapters we will look at the wide spectrum of opportunities that you have to improve the efficiency of your business, but the point to remember here is that it is not simply about profit.

You influence your cash flow by how effectively you go about your day-to-day activities. By becoming more effective and more efficient in what you do, you reduce the time gap between cash going out and cash coming in, as well as cutting out unnecessary cost.

Of course, while cash-flow management can get you through the short term, in the medium and long term your business has got to be profitable. Spend more than you earn and you run out of cash. In the first part of this book, we showed you how to increase your income and boost your top-line revenue. In the following chapters, we'll show you how to increase your profitability by managing your business more effectively.

4. Spending the right money

For most businesses, the main source of funding comes from the bank line of credit. There may have been some additional monies put in by the owner-manager and their family but the reality for most businesses is that this is little more than start-up funding. That's fair enough. We can argue long into the night about the lack of funding available for businesses but we have to deal with the real world.

The bank line of credit is designed to deal with the daily fluctuations in a business's cash flow. We've already written about the cash outflows that hit a business because of the time gap that exists between when you spend your money, on wages, materials and overheads, and when your customer pays you.

Over time this should correct itself. You spend $1,000 putting a job together and receive $1,500 at a later date when the customer pays you.

Of course, by then, you've already spent money on the next job and so the cycle continues.

If your business is settled and profitable, you will end up eventually with increasing funds in the bank at the end of each month.

If your business is growing but still profitable then the point at which the cash starts to accumulate is pushed back as you plow more money in to fund increasing amounts of work. You should still eventually catch up, providing you have sufficient funds to cover the gap in the meantime.

16. Why Do We Keep Running Out Of Cash?

In a nutshell, this is what the bank line of credit is for. It's there to cover the time gap between you paying money out and getting the related sales money back in.

This is a good example of why maintaining cash-flow forecasts is so important. If you don't know the size of the gap, in both time and monetary terms, then you don't know what size of line of credit you require.

One reason why busy and profitable businesses still run out of cash is because they've tried to operate with an insufficient line of credit facility and that is because they haven't tracked their needs. Here's a simple example:

A business produces 100 jobs per month at a cost of $50 per job and a sale price of $150 with one month's credit. They invoice at the month-end but receive no credit. Here's the first six months' figures:

	Mth 1	Mth 2	Mth 3	Mth 4	Mth 5	Mth 6
	$	$	$	$	$	$
Units	100	100	100	100	100	100
Sales	15,000	15,000	15,000	15,000	15,000	15,000
Costs	5,000	5,000	5,000	5,000	5,000	5,000
Profit	10,000	10,000	10,000	10,000	10,000	10,000
Cash	(5,000)	10,000	10,000	10,000	10,000	10,000
Bank	(5,000)	5,000	15,000	25,000	35,000	45,000

A cash deficit is created at the end of month 1 as the production costs are met but the sales invoices face the credit delay. However, a steady profit of $10,000 a month quickly turns the cash shortfall into a healthy balance. By the end of month 2 the business is cash-rich. The $5,000 short-term line of credit provided by the bank is sufficient to ride the early pressure.

Now compare this with a business selling the same product but expanding rapidly...

	Mth 1	Mth 2	Mth 3	Mth 4	Mth 5	Mth 6
	$	$	$	$	$	$
Units	100	500	2,000	5,000	10,000	20,000
Sales	15,000	75,000	300,000	750,000	1,500,000	3,000,000
Costs	5,000	25,000	100,000	250,000	500,000	1,000,000
Profit	10,000	50,000	200,000	500,000	1,000,000	2,000,000
Cash	(5,000)	(10,000)	(25,000)	50,000	250,000	500,000
Bank	(5,000)	(15,000)	(40,000)	10,000	260,000	760,000

The business is generating a profit to die for and, ultimately, a bank balance to match. Look, however, at what has happened to the cash in the early months. The rapid expansion has meant that cash is leaving the business far quicker than it is coming in.

The gap between rapidly growing production costs being paid and the benefit of the sales coming in has generated a $40,000 cash deficit by month 3, despite the company having accumulated profits of $200,000 by that time.

For a well-managed business, properly prepared with financial forecasts, this is unlikely to be a problem. Having identified the cash requirement early and approached the bank properly, the funding is in place and things are looking good.

However, go back to our first business with the $5,000 facility. If they experienced a similar sort of growth, where would they be with their $5,000 facility? The likelihood is that the business would not get as far as the good times, with bank and creditor pressure being, at best, a major headache and, at worst, fatal.

Combine good financial forecasting with line of credit borrowing and you have the flexibility to finance your growth, providing you are aware of your needs in advance and act accordingly.

Where a line of credit can quickly go wrong is when it is used to fund something that it wasn't designed for. What would have happened to the business above if it had purchased a machine for $5,000 in month 1 to speed up production? Immediately, it puts itself in a financial predicament, having used up all its financial options in one shot.

The funding should match the benefits. A line of credit deals with the daily fluctuations in a business but can be swallowed up by capital purchases like a machine or vehicle.

The important factor here is that such items have a longer impact on a business and therefore should have financial solutions that match. Using funding options such as loans, hire purchase, lease purchase or contract hire, in other words options spread over a period to match the usefulness of the asset, makes much more sense and keeps your line of credit or cash funds clear for the daily needs.

Always try to ensure that you protect the liquid funds in your business by not tying them up into longer-term assets.

5. Be conservative with the benefits

Sometimes, owner-managers simply take too much cash out of the business.

How much you pay yourself is just as much a business decision as any other cost. You cannot allow personal financial demands to dictate the draw policy that you have. If your business cannot sustain the level of draws that you absolutely need, then you either need to quickly improve your performance or accept that you can't make it work and get out.

This may sound heartless but it is reality. If you allow your business to fail because you've taken out more than it can afford, then you are cheating your creditors, and quite possibly, breaking the law.

More often the problem can arise through simply not being aware of all the implications, especially the tax effect.

If you run an unincorporated business, most commonly a sole proprietor or partnership, then you will pay yourself draws out of the profits that arise. However, those profits are also giving rise to a tax liability at a later date. Draw out all the profit and you have nothing left to cover the subsequent tax bill. Always factor in a provision for the tax to be paid.

If you have your own corporation, then you'll be taking at least some of your money out by way of salary. This is easier in some respects because the Internal Revenue Service ensures that you deduct tax as you go along, effectively factoring in the provision.

Dividends are a popular choice for many in order to help minimize their tax. However, once you become a higher-rate taxpayer, these again generate a tax bill down the line which needs to be factored into your cash-flow projections.

The profit that remains in the company faces a similar situation with its Income Tax bill.

It doesn't stop there. For a sales tax-registered business, your customers pay you inclusive of the sales tax, which must subsequently be paid to the appropriate state. The temptation to spend it before then can be immense, once the cash has hit your bank account and there are bills to be paid. It's tough, but creating a sales tax reserve in order to put the monies aside for the sales tax return is good financial management and will help the business to avoid overspending.

So, always factor tax arrangements into your forecasts when planning your own compensation and the business's wider spending.

6. Plan for what can't be planned for

Things go wrong. No matter how well you manage your business, there are always going to be external forces and actions that you cannot prevent. From the well-executed crime, through accident and bad-luck to large-scale economic crash, some things you cannot be held accountable for.

But you can still give yourself a chance. Businesses require prudence as well as risk-taking. Keeping some back for a rainy day may be an old-fashioned ideal but it could just save you one day.

So, let's just summarize the key points in our cash management:

- Cash-flow forecasts are a vital cash management tool. You cannot manage effectively without it.

- Effective credit control starts from the beginning of the customer relationship and not from when the invoice has become overdue.

- The efficiency of your business processes and the health of your cash balance go hand-in-hand.

- Understand your finance options and choose wisely.

- Don't neglect the tax.

- Plan for the unexpected.

It's board meeting time. What are our two firms doing about their cash position?

Black & Grey Widgets

Of course Black & Grey know that cash is tight but isn't it for everyone at the moment? The partners are aware that the amount owed by customers is getting bigger but they don't want to lose any customers by getting too tough with them. They agree to make a few phone calls.

They're having to juggle the creditors a bit at the moment but that'll get better when the orders pick up. There's no need to panic.

They agree to have a look at their costs to see what savings they can make that will help but there's not much more they feel they can do at the moment and so they move on to the next item.

Rainbow Widgets

"So having revised the forecasts for last month's actual results, we've got a clear plan for our payments over the next month. Borrowing is sufficient, so no problems there. The debtors are coming down now that our manager has reminded a few of them about our terms and conditions.

"The reduced production times last month have made a big difference and we're up to date with all our bills now. Next month's sales tax is covered and the agreement for the purchase on the new machine has been signed off, so we're moving ahead as planned."

Key Summary & Action Points

1. Re-read this section to fully understand why your cash position isn't better than it is.

2. Take responsibility for the position your business is in. You have to start somewhere and so better management starts today.

3. Understand that as long as you have the right attitude (this WILL work for me rather than this will never work in my business) you can change your circumstances.

Why Businesses Stop Growing...

Section 3: Agenda Item 17

17. How Do We Make More Profit?

Introduction

Profit is an outcome. It's the end result of the actions and inactions in your business. If you want to increase your profit, then you need to do things better than you have before. You need to be more effective and more efficient across all aspects of your business.

Easy.

If only it was!

Because profit is an outcome, then, every action recommended in this book is relevant and has a positive impact on profit. Rather than have you re-read every page, though (not a bad idea, mind), let's look at the fundamentals of increasing profit.

The first thing to remember is that there is rarely a single, magic solution to dramatically increasing your profit. It can happen, but more often than not, increasing your profit is about doing many small things better than you have in the past. Too often, businesses fail to maximize their profit because they ignore the small changes in their hunt for the one that makes a big impact. Those small changes, all added together and having an increasing impact as time goes by, quite often <u>are the big impact</u>.

Let's go back to the three core components of any business that we discussed at the start of this book and again at the start of this section.

Management is how well and effectively you run your business. Process is what you actually do, your products or services. Sales and marketing is who you sell it to, in what quantities and at what price. We can look at profit through these three components.

Sales and marketing	=	Revenue
Process	=	Costs
Management	=	Best value

We've previously discussed the need to address all three components of a business in relative measures if that business is to grow successfully. Focusing primarily on process, as many businesses do, stifles growth because the lack of attention to the management and sales and marketing components adds barriers.

So it is with profit maximization. Focusing in isolation on growing the top line, or on cutting costs, can bring short-term benefits but in the longer term can be counter-productive. Too many customers can increase non-recoverable costs such as overtime, returns, overstocking, etc. Cutting costs too far can restrict profit through lack of resources, poor-quality product, and so on.

Profit maximization has to therefore be approached in as much of a strategic fashion as your business's growth plans. In this book, we have shown you, over and over again, how to get more of the customers and sales that you want. The emphasis, you will notice, has always been on getting the <u>right</u> sort of customers and the <u>right</u> sales in a <u>cost-effective</u> manner. Rather than looking at increasing your revenue, the focus of the sales and marketing strategies that we recommend looks at a much more rounded approach, bringing in the management and cost strategies of the business:

Don't get any customer... get the right one at the right price and sell them the right things.

You see how this is a much more encompassing approach but also the most profitable. You are not wasting money on badly thought-out and poorly executed sales and marketing approaches that run the risk of bringing in non-profitable customers.

Anyone can pick up new business. Dramatically undercut all of your competitors and massively advertise the fact and you'll get loads of new customers... but will you make more profit? Only if this is a carefully considered strategy and one that ties in with your management and process strategies. In other words, high volume and hugely efficient in everything you do. If that's not your business, then such a marketing approach would have a devastating impact on profit.

So, before you set about increasing your profit, you have to make sure that you fully understand all three components of your business strategy:

Process	What do we do best, what can we do and what shouldn't we do?

Sales and marketing	Who are our customers and what do they want?
Management	Who are we, what are we and where are we going?

Once you are confident in your ability to answer these questions, then, and only then, are you in a position to really set about increasing your profitability.

1.   Increasing your profit from sales and marketing

You'll notice that we've deliberately not headed this as 'increasing your revenue'. It may be the answer but not necessarily so. Remember, sell the right things to the right people in the right quantities for your business.

In this book to date we've given you everything that you need to know and do in order to increase your profit from sales and marketing.

So, this is the easy bit. You're either now doing it or, at the very least, you have the roadmap showing you how.

If you don't have the answer now, go back to the beginning and read it all again... seriously!

2.   Increasing your profit by controlling your costs

Again, you'll notice we've not headed this as 'cutting your costs'. There may be times in any business when you just have to save the cash and cut your costs but that's a reaction, not a strategy. If it has to be done, then it has to be done, but it should never be anything more than a short-term survival measure.

In the same way that your sales and marketing is most profitable if it is planned in a controlled manner that is right for your business as a whole, so your cost control will have the most beneficial impact on the profitability of your business if it is done on a more rounded basis and not just focused on cutting costs.

In essence, this means getting the most benefit per dollar spent. It's better to spend $10 on something that will generate $20 of profit than it is to save $4 in the short term by spending $6 on something that generates only $8 in profit.

A 100% return on the more expensive unit compared to a 33% on the cheaper version...providing, of course, that you don't just have $6 to spend in the first place.

This is where budgeting is so important. We covered this in the previous chapter, and financial forecasts have to be the starting point for any cost control. You have to know what money you have to play with and how you intend to allocate it.

With your forecasts in place, look at how much funds you've allocated to each specific cost and then set about achieving the best value that you can, i.e. the most benefit to your business, from those funds. Remember that you are looking at it in the round and not just with the tunnel vision of saving money.

The Hunt for Best Value

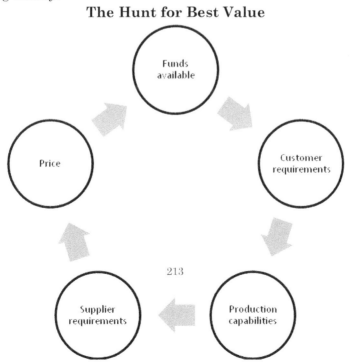

For each area of cost, you are looking not at what you could potentially save on price but what is available out there in the market place that will enable you to deliver what your customers want at the most effective price for your budget.

Go back to our example. If your budget allows you to spend $10 per unit and this delivers what your customers want for the most profit ($20), then this is the direction you clearly go.

However, if your budget doesn't allow you to spend $10, if it doesn't deliver what your customers want, if your people can't make it work or if it simply isn't available out there in the market place, then it's back to the drawing board.

Maybe the $6 product is now your answer, but again, only if it delivers what your customers want and there is nothing more effective out there in the market place.

It's a matter of:

- Knowing your budget

- Understanding your customers' needs

- Understanding your own limitations and skills

- Knowing your supplier options

All of these are constantly moving pictures so cost control is not a once-a-year exercise and this is often where the avoidable costs start to creep in. Business owners will often source a supplier and then, providing the service remains reasonable, stay with them for many years without revisiting what is happening in either the supplier or customer market place.

Loyalty is a big thing. We look for it from our customers and our suppliers should be looking for the same.

We're not advocating a constantly changing supplier list but it is important that your suppliers earn your loyalty by staying at the forefront of their market and continuing to supply you with the best possible deal out there.

It is fair for you to revisit your arrangements on a regular basis to ensure that you are still getting best value for your spend. Loyalty doesn't have to come at a price.

This brings another factor into play. Part of your equation is to ensure that you are sourcing supplies that help you deliver what your customer wants.

How does your supplier know what your customer wants?

How do you know if your supplier could help you better deliver what your customer wants?

The fact is, unless you bring your supplier into the loop of understanding that you have of your customer's needs, then you run the risk of missing out on an opportunity to deliver it better.

The price, quality, quantity and timing of delivery of your products and services to your customers are affected, directly and indirectly, by the price, quality, quantity and timing of delivery of your suppliers' products and services to you.

The better your suppliers understand your needs AND the needs of your customers, the more chance you have of the whole process being effective. Of course, you have to be aware of any competitive elements and of any customer confidentiality needs, but it's worthwhile looking at your list of suppliers to see and judge who you can bring closer to your business and your customer's business for the benefit of you all.

Clearly, most businesses will have a wide range of suppliers:

- Small suppliers with a close relationship

- Suppliers with little relationship

- Large suppliers

- Regular suppliers

- Intermittent suppliers

- Key accounts

- 'Monopoly' suppliers

Cost control is not a 'one size fits all' approach. Determining the nature of the relationship, the degree of dependency and the suitability of resource is down to the experience of the business owner and will influence just how much communication is possible and worthwhile.

We've not made reference yet to what, for many businesses, is their biggest cost... staff. Your workforce are suppliers like the rest of your purchase ledger, and in many respects, the same principles apply. Getting the best value from your payroll depends, in part at least, on similar factors:

- Understanding the requirements and skills of your staff

- Getting the most effective price level

- Understanding the staff market

- Ensuring staff understand your needs and those of your customers

We'll discuss the whole subject of staff performance later.

This is a different slant on cost control, then. No longer are we looking at simply the cheapest option. Instead you run down your profit and loss account with a quite different checklist in place:

- Is this item of expenditure in line with budget?

- Is this line of expenditure necessary?

- Am I best meeting my customers' needs in this area?

- Have the terms and conditions of this supplier been reviewed recently?

- Is there scope for working more closely with this supplier?

- What else is out there?

- Can I simply cut the cost without affecting my customers?

We advocate a systemized process for everything. Cost control is no different.

You should establish a timetable for reviewing your costs in line with this checklist. How regularly and extensively will depend on the resources you have to hand.

If it's just you, then split your overheads into small groups and tackle a few every month. If you have some people available, then have either one person allocated to control the cost as a key function of their job or allocate the costs to different people according to their function.

However you do it, regular and systematic review within the framework of the checklist above will enable you to use cost control as a means of increasing customer service and increasing profitability at the same time.

3. Increasing your profit by improving your management.

We've looked at the sales and cost factors of profit. In both cases, it's been a matter of looking at how those areas can be improved within the framework of the entire business and not just in isolation.

We've improved the profitability of our sales and marketing effectively by understanding our market place better.

We've improved the effectiveness of the dollars that we spend by taking what we know of our customers and looking at our supplies in that context.

So let's now look at the bit in between. Let's look at what happens when we better manage the processes that we control.

This may seem like a blindingly obvious statement but your business has more chance of being more profitable if you manage it more effectively.

For a blindingly obvious statement, this is probably the greatest failing in most businesses today.

Ever heard the statement about "working on your business and not in it"? Of course you have. Do you follow it through?

The fact is that the vast majority of people managing small businesses today started that business NOT because they wanted to run a business but because they wanted to do what they do their way.

In other words, they were employed as an engineer but thought they knew a better way to be an engineer. They were employed as a designer but thought they knew a better way to be a designer. Sound familiar?

The driving force was to do a job a different way or to service customers a different way and the only way to do it was to set up on their own. Absolutely nothing wrong with this, we've pretty much all done it.

The problem is that we end up with really good engineers and really good designers trying to do a job they've not been trained for, which is to run a business.

We could write a book on this issue alone but let's look at it in the context of what we are talking about here. If you are going to make a profit, then you have to do what you do in the most efficient and effective manner.

If you use other people, systems and processes to do what you do, then you have to ensure that they all work in the most efficient and effective manner.

But we've all been trained as engineers, designers, etc. We've not been trained to manage processes and people. Okay, we can overcome that in the same way that we overcome most things in business and that's by using the experience and expertise that we've gathered, and by using the experience and expertise of others to address the issue in the best manner.

However, if we don't take the time to step back and look at our businesses from this perspective, if we continue to work in the business as designers, engineers or whatever, instead of working on it as managers, then our expertise and experience is one-dimensional and does nothing for the overall efficiency and effectiveness.

Here's what you have to do:

- Have a plan for your business: a map so you know where you're trying to go. We've already stressed the need for financial forecasts. You can't really have one without the other.

- Identify the key information that you need to run your business and put in place a means by which you can readily extract this. It could be financial (cash received, profit, etc.), it could be process-based (units produced, wastage, etc.), it could be customer-focused (number of new customers, average spend, number of complaints, etc.). It probably should be a mixture of all three. Whatever the fundamental information you need to best measure the current performance of your business, you must have it to hand.

- Allocate a specific half day or day every month when you focus on the management of your business and nothing else. Put it in your calendar every month for the year ahead and have it cast in stone.

  Get away from the office or lock your door, turn off your mobile phone and disconnect your laptop. Allow nothing to distract you from focusing <u>on</u> your business. Have a fixed agenda, have your key information available, and as a minimum, cover:

- Finance (cash flow and profit)

- Sales and Marketing

- Workflow management

- Staff performance and development

- Customers' issues

Nobody is expecting you to be Sir Alan Sugar. It's a matter of creating a moment each month when your mind is focused solely on running your business. Then you can return to the fire-fight knowing what the bigger picture looks like.

• Actively manage your team. Fans of "Hill Street Blues", the brilliant cop series of the 90s, will remember the routine at the start of every shift when the sergeant would gather the watch together, run through everyone's duties, give out the messages and then finish in fatherly tones with, "Hey, let's be careful out there".
This is what you need to do with your team, every Monday morning. Make sure everyone is informed, coordinated and up for the fight.

• Plan your work. The temptation is always to get on with the job but 5 minutes of planning saves hours of wasted work and dollars of lost profit. Make sure you record it, too, as a point of reference.

• Review your processes. Firstly, because you shouldn't assume that the way you think things are being done is actually the way they are being done. Secondly, because the fact that something has always been done that way isn't a reason why it's the best way to do it in the future.

- Always be business-like. Of course you want to do the best possible job for your customers but look at the task from your perspective as well. Where could this go wrong? How could we lose money? Most importantly, how do we go about the job and its paperwork so that we cover these risks?

- Have a plan for continually training and developing your staff. If you simply continue to do what you've always done, and if your training is restricted to the internal passing on of knowledge, then the lack of ideas from outside is going to see your skills level gradually deteriorate. You and your team need to get out there, see what's happening in the rest of the world, learn new skills and keep on progressing.

Let's summarize what we are saying here.

If you want to increase your profits, then the historical equation has been simple, at least in theory:

- Increase your sales by selling more often to more people at a higher price.

- Reduce your overheads by cutting costs.

Our argument is that this is too simplistic and potentially damaging. Profit is an outcome of all the functions of a business. To improve it, you are therefore looking to improve a series of linked processes, and understanding the links and ensuring consistent actions is much more important. The way to increase your profit is therefore:

- Improve the effectiveness of your sales and marketing strategy by following the approach we detail in this book.

- Improve the return on what you spend your budget on, getting more value per dollar spent in all areas.

- Manage your business more effectively. An old cliché but too important to ignore...<u>Work on it, not in it.</u>

What's happening in our board rooms?

Black & Grey Widgets

Profits have flat-lined but that's to be expected in the current economic climate, isn't it? The partners want to act before the situation deteriorates, though. They don't feel that a price increase is going to go down well with their customers so they need to look at the costs instead.

They agree to carry out a review of salaries and staffing levels and look for savings from their suppliers. They also recognize that they may need to look elsewhere to make savings.

Rainbow Widgets

"The reduced production times that we brought in to improve our cash flow are also having a positive impact on profit. This is combining with the excellent results that we are getting from the more effective marketing strategies we've applied, to give us record profits for this stage of the year. We're ahead of forecast, and given what we know about our future forecasts and budgets, we're in a position to consider a bonus for the team.

"It's true what they say... manage your business effectively and profit will take care of itself."

Key Summary & Action Points

1. Re-read this section to fully understand the link between effective management and profit.

2. Understand that profit is an outcome and not a section of your business to be viewed in isolation.

3. Greater efficiency and smarter management = more profit.

18. How Do We Find The Time To Do Things Better?

Introduction

Ask a business owner-manager what they would like more of and the answer that you get, over and over again, is "more time, please". It's hugely frustrating for many people to be aware of the things that they need to address in their business and to have plans for improving it, but to be prevented from doing so by not having the time... and knowing that the situation will only get worse.

What would you do if you had more time?

- Spend more time looking after your customers?

- Spend more time training and developing both you and your team?

- Spend more time developing products and ideas?

- Spend more time managing the performance of the business?

- Spend more time with friends and family?

- Spend more time doing what you enjoy?

...All of the above?

Being short of time damages you and your business, doesn't it? So we have to find ways of creating more time in your business. Let's start with you.

225

Why Businesses Stop Growing...

If you want to create more time for yourself, then you have to be prepared to be more formal, more disciplined, and most importantly, more committed to yourself. The demands made on your time bear down on you from a multitude of directions:

- Clients and customers

- Staff

- Suppliers

- Internal Revenue Service

- United States Government

- Local Government

- Landlord

- Bank

- Insurers

- Professional & business bodies

- Sales people

...and the list goes on.

Last but not least: your family and friends

...and finally

...**YOU!**

These are not people who you can afford to ignore, although it's fair to say that some have a more legitimate claim on your time than others. You shouldn't turn your back on customers, staff, suppliers, family and yourself, for instance, but you ignore the others at your peril.

The trick is to take charge of your time in such a way that you can give priority to those that really matter, delegate those that can be passed down, and control the expectations, demands and access of all.

The best way to start is to look at your non-productive manager time. We first should define what we mean by this.

Non-productive manager time is the time that you spend on doing stuff that you don't want to do and can't make any money doing. In other words, think about all the things you enjoy doing at work and all the things that make you good money, and non-productive manager time is everything else.

Now we have to analyze this.

Grab a piece of paper and head up three columns:

Things I've Got To Do	Things I Want To Do	Stuff To Delegate
{Column 1}	{Column 2}	{Column 3}

Now start to run through all the things that you do in your working day and enter each task into the relevant column.

In column 1 you enter those tasks that only you can do. We don't mean the tasks that only you in your business can do, but only YOU can do.

Quite often these will be determined by matters of confidentiality or because they are of a personal nature. The fact is that whether you want to do these particular tasks or not, it isn't appropriate, practical or possible to give them to anyone else, either inside or outside your business. This is the stuff that only the owner or boss can do.

In column 2 you enter the tasks that you want to do. A really simple point of principle applies here. It's your business. What's the point of having your own business if you can't do what you want to do, within legal reason, of course? In this column you enter the reasons why you come to work, the things that motivate and challenge you, the things that you just love to do. This is the list that will set your goals for your dream job in your business. Don't let practical realities restrict you at this stage. The fact that you are unable to do what you want at the moment doesn't prevent you from putting it on to your list. Remember, an aim of this approach is to unlock your time. What you don't plan for, you are unlikely to achieve.

Finally, if it doesn't have to go into column 1 and you don't want it to go into column 2, then it goes into column 3. This is the dumping ground, the stuff you don't have to do or want to do.

Now let's set about clearing column 3.

What we've done is create a list of tips and proven techniques for doing just that. The more you apply, the better you'll control your time and the more you will free yourself from your business.

Here we go...

1. Delegate

Delegation is the most effective way of shifting work off your desk, yet we constantly hear from business managers that they are unable to do so. Most commonly, they feel that they can't trust their staff or they don't have staff with the necessary skills or expertise.

Let's tackle this head-on. If you don't trust your staff, then you shouldn't employ them. If they don't have the necessary skills, then you should ensure that they gain sufficient training to give them their skills.

The real reason is that, while owner-managers complain about their workload, they don't actively develop their staff because, for the most part, they are control freaks and they don't want to relinquish this control.

When an owner-manager says that "it is easier to do the job myself", they are actually saying that they are more comfortable being a worker than a manager. They would sooner restrict the performance and growth of their business by acting like sole proprietors than by properly planning and managing the recruitment and development of their staff.

A staff member will rarely approach work in the same manner as you. Their motivation is completely different. In a recent spot survey we carried out, more than 81% of employees said that they came to work because they needed the money. That isn't to say that they are not motivated or committed, merely that they don't approach work with the same mentality as you.

So, accept that an employee isn't a mini-version of you. Accept that they won't necessarily approach a task and carry it out in exactly the same way as you would. Does that mean that what they are doing is wrong? Clearly, not necessarily.

With motivated, well-trained, disciplined and informed staff, you have the opportunity to delegate large quantities of the work in your category list. Without them, you don't have the same options. But you're the boss. If they are going to be motivated, well trained, disciplined and informed, then it has to come from you.

And it won't happen overnight. In the short term, it is another task in your column 1 but it will lead to significant delegation opportunity and so it has to be tackled.

The key to successful delegation isn't just having the people to delegate to. Once those people are in place, you still have to manage them. This falls into three stages:

Plan:	Make sure they know what is expected of them.
Control:	Make sure they have appropriate support and supervision.
Review:	Make sure the outcome is checked and feedback is given.

Delegation isn't about dumping work on other people. It's about ensuring that the right work is given to the appropriate staff members in a fashion that's planned and controlled so they understand your expectations and requirements, have the time and skills to address them, and then produce work to a standard that you are reasonably entitled to expect from the training and support they have received.

This may seem time-consuming but it's much more time-effective than doing every task yourself. It's certainly the main way to remove the greatest barrier to the growth of your business, which is a shortage of your time.

So, for effective delegation...

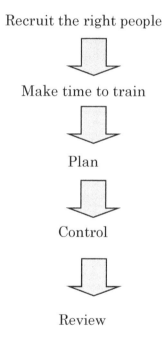

Recruit the right people

Make time to train

Plan

Control

Review

...or do it all yourself until you run out of will!

2.   Outsource

When you genuinely don't have the people available within your own enterprise to enable you to delegate a task, the next place to look is outside your four walls. "Is there anyone out there who I can pay to do the job for me?"

Thanks to the internet as much as anything else, you can pretty much find a solution to whatever service you are looking for these days. The issues to consider are:

- Cost

- Control

- Security

Business managers who find it easier to "do it myself" than to delegate also tend to prefer to "do it myself rather than pay somebody else to". Both attitudes can be equally short-sighted. In the current economic situation, nobody should be incurring unnecessary costs but it's a matter of weighing up the overall benefits to your business.

Let's look at an example. This is a small engineering company with an owner-manager and six staff, all production.

It works with limited resources and is under pressure with both workflow and cash flow. The boss needs to keep his staff fully employed to meet both needs, as well as be as productive as possible himself.

The effectiveness of his own production is affected by constant interruptions as he deflects all other tasks from the staff. Business management is extremely limited by his lack of time. The business can't afford a full-time administrator.

It's a scenario you are highly likely to recognize in your own business.

After much persuasion, and almost as a desperate measure to get work done, the boss finally Googles for office support. He finds that there are companies out there who will answer his phone during busy periods, collate and prioritize e-mails, provide secretarial support and offer a host of wider support options for less than the cost of one lost day of his production time each month.

It's a no-brainer.

Should've done it years ago.

The added cost of the bought-in support is heavily outweighed by the benefits to the business of freeing up his production and management time. Cash flow as well as workflow sees a positive swing even though the company is spending more money.

As well as being cost-effective, the outsourcing needs to be controlled and controllable.

The object of the exercise is to free up your time to better manage the business.

Clearly this isn't going to happen if you are spending even more time sorting out any problems generated by the arrangement.

You should be happy that the terms enhance both your internal operations and the service that your customers receive. It's worth spending time at the outset to ensure that the supplier's culture and mind-set fits in with your own. You need to be confident that they properly understand your business and the needs and expectations of you and your customers.

You can expect to have to make some changes to your own procedures to accommodate the new arrangements but you should again be confident that these enhance your operation and aren't a matter of you changing the way you do things simply to fit in with the supplier's way.

It should feel like a genuine relationship, a true partnership. Ask yourself three key questions:

- Do they understand my business needs?

- Do they understand my customers' expectations?

- Am I benefitting from changes I have to make?

The final area to consider is security. This covers two different types of security. The first is the security of your intangible assets, things like:

- Your name and reputation

- Your customer list

- Your intellectual property

- Your staff goodwill

You don't want to bring in an outsource partner who is going to damage or steal any of these. For instance, credit control and accounts receivable management is an area commonly outsourced but you may not wish to partner up with a firm who has a reputation for sending Uncle Vito in to collect.

In another instance, you wouldn't want to bring in a firm who had a hidden agenda for your customer list.

Your gut reaction will always be a guide but you should also do your own research. Ask around, check out the internet and seek testimonials and references from existing customers.

The second area of security is almost security of tenure. It could backfire on you to outsource an operation to a company that goes out of business six months later or has a reputation for chopping and changing its business deals.

Again, check them out. Do a credit check, look into their business history and interrogate them on other business relationships that they've had.

3. Eliminate the time wasters

Previously in this book we've introduced you to the different customer types that exist in most businesses. Let's revisit that diagram...

```
           ┌─────────────────┬─────────────────┐
           │                 │                 │
R          │  'B+' Customers │                 │
E          │                 │                 │
L          │                 │  'A' Customers  │
A          │                 │                 │
T          │  'B' Customers  │                 │
I          │                 │                 │
O          ├─────────────────┼─────────────────┤
N          │                 │                 │
S          │                 │                 │
H          │                 │                 │
I          │  'D' Customers  │  'C' Customers  │
P          │                 │                 │
           │                 │                 │
           └─────────────────┴─────────────────┘
```

PROFIT

'A' customers are your best customers, lovely people spending good money with you.

'B' customers are your most common customer. Lovely people, not spending as much as you'd like but restricted by budget usually. Within them are the 'B+' customers for whom this is a temporary restriction and they have the potential to become 'A's.

'C' and 'D' customers are both negative customers, with the only difference being that you do make money out of your 'C's.

Let's look at 'C's and 'D's more closely. What are common characteristics of these types of customer?

- They don't respond to communications

- They leave everything until the last minute

- They never tell you what's going on

- They never work as agreed

- They forever change their mind

- They upset staff

- They complain about everything

- They demand instant attention

- They pester you

- They haggle over prices

- Their own administration is poor

- They don't listen to advice

- They always look to blame you

How much of this is a waste of your time?

All of it!

The solution?

Don't allow 'C' and 'D' customers to exist in your business!!

Put them right. And if they won't be put right, then sell them, sack them, out-price them or whatever but don't allow them to torment your business any longer.

They may make a contribution to your cash flow and revenue but the time and energy that you waste in trying to keep them happy can always be better spent. Better spent on management, sales and marketing, and business improvement.

If the cash-flow impact of losing these customers in the short term is significant, then you don't need to be gung-ho about it.

Equally, you don't need to keep them forever. The important thing is to identify them, work out when is the best time to lose them with the minimum hit on cash flow, and work to that plan.

Another way to do it is to use them as a reward program. Every time you hit target, or gain new business, use it as an excuse to give one of your 'C' or 'D' customers the boot.

Double the celebration!

4.   Be an Enforcer

Part of your job, as boss if you like, is to ensure that other people actually do their jobs. This is one of those areas where it's often easier to see from an outsider's perspective whether it is being done effectively or not.

Owner-managers tend to be control freaks. In general, they also have a different perspective and a raised expectation on the performance and standards of their business and the levels of customer service they should deliver.

We've already said that the majority of employees come to work to earn money. It's a different motivation.

This can sometimes backfire on the diligent owner-manager. Because everything means more, there's a danger of becoming a backstop or goalkeeper for the business. For example...

- If something doesn't get finished, then not to worry because you will finish it.

- If nobody else likes doing something, then not to worry because you will do it.

- If an individual is uncomfortable about part of their role, then not to worry because you will take it off them.

Familiar?

How many times do you end up doing something that an employee should've done and, actually, is paid to do?

The fact is that you have to enforce your role and make sure that others carry out tasks and responsibilities that are part of the job that you pay them to do. Some people are uncomfortable with this while others fall back into the "quicker to do it myself" syndrome.

We're not advocating a "Just Do It" approach, at least not in this case. You clearly have a responsibility to ensure that people are properly trained and supported in what they do and properly remunerated for doing so. But, once you have fulfilled your responsibilities as a good employer, it is right and proper of you to expect and, indeed, demand that your team fulfill their responsibilities as employees.

There is a straightforward mind-set to establish here as 'boss'.

"I am going to do my job properly. Part of my doing my job properly is to be a good employer and to ensure that others are good employees. I'm not doing my job properly if I allow others not to do their job properly, not to earn their pay.... So, I am going to do my job."

5. De-clutter

Clear-desk policy, tidying up, getting rid of the clutter, call it what you like. Having a tidy workplace and tidy work area saves time. Time lost in losing things, forgetting things, damaging things, duplicating tasks, stressing over work piles, losing one's way and generally being as ineffective and inefficient as man can be.

It's such a simple solution, getting staff and yourself to put things away, yet it is one of the greatest time-savers and stress-busters.

A tidy bench is a tidy mind.

A tidy desk is a tidy mind.

It doesn't matter what your environment is, keeping it tidy makes you more effective.

This time we are saying...."Just Do It!"

6. Take control of your day, week, month and year

Much of your time is lost in interruptions. These are quite often for valid reasons by staff, customers and other callers, but they break your concentration and break up your day. Telephone calls, e-mails, mail, appointments and face-to-face callers are a double-edged sword. Without them you probably don't have a business, but with them you have your main headache.

So take control.

You need vacations. You cannot perform at your best week after week after week. Your first task every new year should be to block out some vacation time in your calendar. Once they're in there, you can plan your workloads around them and make customers and staff aware. Wait until work permits and you'll never get away.

With your vacations booked, we can now take it a step further. What days and hours are you prepared to work as a norm? If you don't want to work Sundays or evenings, for example, then make it a rule, make sure your staff is aware and build it into your work plans. Only YOU have the power to break your rules!

Now let's look at your days. What's your maximum number of meetings in a day, for instance, or in a week? What is the earliest you are prepared to have a meeting? What days are best kept clear? Make the rules.

This framework for your working life is vital.

For most of us, the right work-life balance is important but a struggle to achieve, and work is usually the dominant partner. Setting a framework for your working life is the only way to bring it under control, but also a benchmark to judge your business by.

If you aren't able to make your business work to your rules within a reasonable time frame, say two years, then you must question whether you are doing the right thing by continuing it. Is your business the right thing for your life?

Let's move on to those interruptions.

It's important for any business to be accessible to its customers but you can control it. Take e-mails as an example.

E-mails constantly interrupt what you do. They have no manners whatsoever.

A common mistake is to deal with an e-mail there and then, to get it out of the way, if you like. The problem is that this raises an expectation of an immediate reply in the mind of the sender. How much easier would your life be if that expectation was to receive a reply within one working day, for instance, or within 3 hours?

You have to set the expectation.

Our advice is easy to apply and very effective...

Simply switch off your e-mails.

Only open them once or twice a day, at controlled times and times that better suit you, and deal with them then. Stop the interruptions.

Or have someone else manage your e-mails for you. People recoil in horror when this is suggested but think about how many of the e-mails really, really have to be dealt with by you. To have someone filter your e-mails first and only pass on to you those that seriously need your attention WILL save you hours each week.

Phone calls need to receive the same treatment. When you are in a meeting and can't take a phone call, the world doesn't usually come to an end.

So, again, allocate times of the day when you are simply 'in a meeting'. The balance is important so that you remain accessible to customers but you don't have to drop everything every time the phone rings.

Mail? Easy. Have someone filter it.

Finally, staff. Try to work into your timetable planned times for seeing your staff. This could be a daily walk around your premises. It could be a formal 'open door' time. Most importantly, make sure that staff are aware of your calendar and workload and sympathetic to it.

As we said earlier, only you have the power to break the rules. Only you really know what matters and what doesn't, what takes priority. You can break any rule to suit circumstance... but no one else can without your permission.

7. Don't be a dinosaur

Modern technology saves time. Use it. The fear of the unknown is the most common reason for delaying common-sense business decisions. How many times have you finally got around to investing in change only for you to think afterwards... "Why didn't we do this months ago?"

Everyone can recount a disaster but you have to prepare properly. Understand:

- What your objective is
- Why you are using that particular technology
- Why you are using that particular supplier
- What you expect to get out of it
- How you plan to measure this
- What the back-up is

Let's now get back into our boardrooms.

Black & Grey Widgets

The problem the partners have at Black & Grey is they are personally rushed off their feet but the staff doesn't seem that busy. Still, there's no one else they feel they can rely on so they come to the conclusion they just need to stop moaning and get on with it.

Rainbow Widgets

"The individual staff development programs are working well and they are now taking on more responsibility.

"The new document management system has made a massive difference, as has sorting out our untidy desks. The new rules for meetings and e-mails are working well, so more time for the marketing again next month.

"Are we still on for that golf break?

"Of course!"

Key Summary & Action Points

1. Build time-saving into your business objectives. Have a plan.

2. Do the simple stuff first.

3. Don't be afraid to invest in your people or your resources in order to save your time.

4. Turn your phone and e-mails off throughout the day to avoid dozens of needless interruptions. This alone will ensure you gain hours each week and uninterrupted time makes you at least twice as effective!

18. How Do We Find The Time?

19. How Do We Get The Best Out Of Our Team?

Introduction

Staff are your greatest asset and biggest headache.

They generate profit but can be your biggest cost. Having staff is a double-edged sword and often a classic case of "Can't live with 'em, can't live without 'em!"

If you have the right team performing to the best of their ability, then your business life is going to be easier and more successful, no question.

Get it wrong, and your staff can cost you your business.

It's a critical area.

The problem is that very few of us are expert in how to recruit, develop, manage, motivate and retain people.

Think of it like a sports team...

You need to spot and buy in the best talent your budget can afford. You need to cover a range of skills. You need to train, guide and motivate your people in order to get the best out of them and you need to find the best team combination.

If you just leave them to play on their own, then you will never get the best results no matter how good they are.

Here are our suggestions, based on practical experience, to at least give you a fighting chance of getting it right...

1. Recruiting The Right People

The most common mistake that's made when a business is looking for staff is that the decision to recruit is delayed and hence the benefit is late in arriving. There are a number of reasons why this is the case, but cost, not having the time to recruit, and fear over workloads dropping off again, tend to be the main ones.

Clearly cost has to be carefully considered but it needs to be measured against the benefits and the cash-flow implications.

You should go back to the section on forecasting because this is where you should start. You need to consider...

- What is this person going to cost me?

- What are the financial and non-financial benefits?

- Can I afford to hire them or, just as importantly, can I afford not to?

Not having the time to recruit is not an acceptable reason, since lack of proper staff may be part of the problem.

You have to make time.

You can always take our advice from earlier and contract out the exercise, possibly using your accountant to evaluate the finances and a recruitment agency to find the person. Yes, it will cost you but go back to the three questions above.

The issue of being overstaffed in the future is again a planning one and a reason to go back to your forecasts. (You'll have gathered by now that all of our advice on running a better business links together like a web. We don't just throw this stuff together!)

You can recruit to fill a space. A job arises in your business, through growth or through a departure, and you set out to find a person to fill it. This reactive approach is probably the most common situation for an employer and is one driven by need.

If you are in this position, don't automatically seek to replace like for like. Look at the implications of the staff change to your wider team structure and make a judgment of your needs on this basis rather than with just the one job in mind. Is it an opportunity for wider restructuring? Can you solve other issues than those created by this single job change?

Try to change a reactive situation into a proactive one.

The main problem with reactive employment is that you are exposed to the variations in the jobs market. You may be seeking staff at the worst possible time to find the right person.

For this reason, there is a growing trend towards proactive recruitment. In other words, you come across the right person, someone who will have a positive impact on your team and your business performance, and you set about creating a role for them.

You still need to ask yourself the same three questions stated above, but you've removed the exposure to employment market variation by attracting talent as you go. In small teams in particular, it is much more important to get the right people than it is to source the most relevant resume.

When it comes to the actual recruitment, most of us, if we're being honest, go by gut reaction. In a small team, that's no bad thing. You can enhance the process by becoming trained in interview and analytical techniques and by becoming more systemized in your recruitment process, but your judgment on how they will 'fit in' remains crucial.

Don't be afraid to be more formal, however. Skills tests, personality tests, trial periods will all tell you something.

Don't choose not to use a head-hunter or recruitment agency simply to avoid the cost. Getting the right person is the overriding factor here, getting the best person for your budget. Getting in the professionals and allowing them to do their job can often be the most effective route to this person.

What matters most is the person. In any business, skills can be taught, personalities are much harder to change.

One last word of advice on recruiting staff...

You should recruit staff based on attitude. If they have the right attitude, you can train them to do anything. A poor attitude cannot be overturned! Don't forget this.

2. Developing Your People

Remember that diagram that we use for analyzing clients? With a few small modifications, it's possible to use the same approach for analyzing and developing your team...

R E L A T I O N S H I P	'B+' Employees 'B' Employees	'A' Employees
	'D' Employees	'C' Employees

PROFIT

'A' employees are your best staff. Great people to work with, excellent ambassadors for the business, good team members, very efficient and very effective.

'B' employees are in many respects your 'typical' employee. Fine to work with, perfectly nice people but not as effective or as efficient as you would wish.

'B+' employees are similar today but are possible rising stars. You see that spark.

'C' employees earn you money but are a problem. Commonly they either fail to follow procedure, upset customers or are disruptive to the team.

'D' employees are even worse. Not only are they disruptive in some way but they have little financial value.

The first thing to do is to plot your staff on to your chart. You have to do this in order to create the right approach towards them. You can't treat all staff the same.

'A' employees need to know they are 'A' employees and be treated as such. You don't want to lose these people. They need training in wider development skills as well as just continuing development of their expertise.

'B+' employees are the same. They need to know their future and have development plans that nurture their talent and ambition.

'B' employees are good people. For whatever reason, this is the limit of their talent or ambition but these are 'engine room' people. They do the job you pay them to and are no hassle.

Their development should ensure that they remain supported and up to date but you need build in no significant further enhancement of their role. The emphasis here should be on developing your systems in order to make them slightly more profitable.

'C' employees earn you money so they deserve one chance but they have to address the issues that sour the relationship, which means that you have to tackle them. If they correct the problem, then you potentially have another 'A' employee. If they refuse or are unable to address the issues, then either you adjust things to solve it from your end (isolate them, for example) or they become a 'D' employee.

'D' employees....Get rid! No excuses, no reason not to.

Every member of your team, apart from the 'D's who you are about to fire, should have a development plan, that you and they work to and that is relevant to their position on your chart.

3. Managing your people

An athlete will run faster if they have a coach. A football team will play better if they have a manager. You will work more effectively in the gym if you have a personal trainer on board.

No matter how motivated a person is, no matter how skilled they are, the right coach is capable of getting something extra out of them.

In your business, you are that coach, manager or trainer. You have to effectively manage your team if you expect to see them perform. That means you have to:

- Plan their roles, responsibilities and duties

- Control their performance

- Review their outcomes

You are therefore looking for the most effective manner in which to do this. Here are some tips:

a) A weekly full-team Monday morning meeting. 15-30 minutes where, as a unit, you discuss the week gone by, the week ahead and other relevant issues. This is essentially a job-planning and motivational half hour designed to make sure everyone knows what's going on and is on-board.

b) A daily 5-minute-per-head walkabout designed to ensure that Monday's plan is unfolding (and not unraveling!)

c) Deadlines should be a feature of every task. Staff should always know what your expectations and requirements are. Open-ended work is never effective.

d) Make bottom-up reporting the norm for your business. In other words, rather than it being up to you to discover what's on track and what isn't, make staff responsible for reporting issues back to you. This requires tasks to be properly planned in the first instance so staff can then accept the plan and the responsibility for delivering it.

e) Provide feedback in a timely manner so staff can absorb it quickly and without the same issues arising on too many tasks in between.

f) Make sure your managers 'manage' (re-read our section on delegation).

4. Motivate Your People

If there is a secret recipe to guarantee 100%-motivated staff then we don't know it! What works in some situations and with some people doesn't work elsewhere. There are general tips that can be applied that make a difference but there is no substitute for knowing your staff.

Everyone has their own style and the trick is to be able to adapt this to suit the person and the circumstance. There is no 'one size fits all' solution so don't waste time looking for one.

Remember also that we've previously discussed why employees come to work. Don't expect "mini-mes". What motivates you won't necessarily motivate them.

While none of the following is likely to be the single solution, all should help raise performance.

- The work environment should be tidy, clean and conducive to good performance. We've discussed having clear-desk/workstation policies before and the concept of tidy workplace/tidy mind. It works.

- Roles and responsibilities should be clear and understood by all. Staff should know what is expected of them and what good performance actually means and what it looks like.

- You should be inclusive. We don't mean open in everything necessarily, this is a matter of style and situation, but if staff is being asked to perform to plan, then they should know what the plan is.

- Lead by example... if this is not obvious, then give up now!

- Support your team. People won't perform if they feel isolated, exposed, put upon or neglected.

- Communicate! Communicate! Communicate! Enough said!

- The issue of staff incentives is a book in its own right so we'll just give you our experiences...

   Staff are motivated primarily by financial return and, secondly, by enjoying their work (i.e. the work environment and the nature of the work). Share-option programs in theory motivate financially but unless the employees can see a direct link between personal performance and financial gain (either capital value or dividend yield) then such programs may have only limited motivational value over a period of time.

   The same applies to profit-sharing programs. The employee has to be able to see the link between their performance and their financial gain if it is to be a true motivator.

   We're not arguing against the use of bonuses, far from it, merely questioning the value of programs that relate to the performance of a group of people rather than an individual.

   Surely an individual is motivated more by a direct link between performance and reward?

   If staff know they are to be rewarded for performance above and beyond that which they are normally remunerated for, then they are more likely to be motivated to achieve it. By avoiding formal programs, employers give themselves the flexibility to properly adjust the reward to suit the performance and the drivers of that individual.

If the main driver for an employee is money, then a lump-sum bonus as a reward for work significantly beyond paid performance will motivate further. Similarly a pay raise for sustained work of this nature is a suitable outcome.

If enjoyment or lifestyle are drivers, then bonus vacation as a reward can have the same impact. More medical coverage for family-orientated staff may work. The key is to understand your staff and motivate them in ways that they see as a direct and valued reward.

Some employers provide a menu of rewards that staff can aim for and choose from. Gifts, activities, time off and bonuses, for example. See what works.

You could always ask them.

You don't necessarily have to always set your targets and rewards high. Staff can be equally motivated by an appreciative boss, customers who value them and colleagues who respect them. Creating a culture of respect and reward goes a long way.

5. Retain Your People

You want staff that your competitors will covet. You have to plan to retain them. Everybody has both a price and a value but follow our guidelines for 1-4 above and you will keep your best people and force your competitors to pay many times over their value to entice them away.

Okay, it's time to see how those boardroom discussions are going...

Black & Grey Widgets

The partners at Black & Grey recognize they need to do something. There is a reluctance to employ anyone new at the moment because of the cost, but they want to be positive and think that some form of profit-related pay program may be worth looking into. They agree to revisit this when they've got a bit more time.

Rainbow Widgets

"We've had a great response from the team again this month. The managers are doing an excellent job and I think we should reward them, both with a one-off bonus and by letting them know that a pay raise is on the way if they can maintain this level. The involvement of the staff in looking at ways of reducing waste has been very positive and we should go with their ideas. Things are looking good for the staff reviews coming up."

Key Summary & Action Points

1. Analyze your staff and put relevant personal development plans into action.

2. Always keep an eye out for good people.

3. Reward exceptional performance.

Why Businesses Stop Growing...

Putting It All Together

The 'Hard' Way Or The 'Easy' Way –
It's Your Choice

Summary

Having read this book, you now realize that to achieve good and consistent results, you need to dedicate sufficient time, effort and expertise.

However, we appreciate that time, knowledge and expertise in marketing and management (especially financial management) are resources which most business owners aren't blessed with, but if you dedicate the time to implementing, learning, testing and generally becoming an expert in both key areas, you can achieve results.

The question we leave you with is this...

Do you have the time to do it all yourself?

If the answer is 'Yes' and you want to go through the process of trial and error, we genuinely wish you great success. You'll need it.

However, if you're like most of the business owners we meet (from start-ups to multi-million-dollar businesses), you're so busy working in the business that the growth and the management of your business, although important to you, often takes a back seat. Sure, things get done intermittently but you're constantly fighting to keep things on track. <u>It's just not that easy</u>.

But there is a better, proven and easier way.

259

You can take the short cut to success.

You can become a client of BHI Bookkeeping, Payroll & Income Tax and immediately start to see results.

You see, we're different. We're not like any other firm of certified public accountants. Of course, like all good accountants, we excel at all the compliance stuff, but there are two things which really set us apart from every other firm...

First, our financial management and tax-saving expertise. You've discovered just from reading this book how our expertise can help you to financially manage the growth of your business. Few accountants are blessed with this kind of real-world expertise.

And second, we invest our own hard-earned money in the 'Business Growth System'. Described by many as the world's leading marketing and business growth program, the Business Growth System has been developed by Steve himself over the last 17 years. It sells for $497 per month but because of our own financial commitment, all our clients get full and FREE access.

As you've just discovered, the combination of sound financial management and the implementation of a sales and marketing system is a potent mix that leads to success.

That's why many of our clients have transformed their fortunes since joining us.

But it takes a certain kind of person and business to ensure our skills and expertise don't go to waste.

And for that reason we don't meet with just anyone.

Nor do we work with everyone who approaches us.

The 'Hard' Way – Or The 'Easy' Way – It's Your Choice

You see, to get results, the business owner(s) need to be ambitious. They must want to build a better business. In fact, they must be driven to continually succeed.

It's these types of people we work with.

It's these types of people who flourish.

It's these types of people who benefit most from our services and our unique approach to accounting.

So if that's you, then we'd be delighted to meet with you.

To arrange your **FREE** one-on-one, no-obligation meeting, simply call us at **702-259-9983**, when we'll explain everything!

Alternatively, you can complete our online form here...

www.Las-Vegas-Business.Com

Thank you.

Why Businesses Stop Growing...

Getting In Touch

The Authors Can Be Contacted In Several Ways

Contacting The Authors:

Brent, Richard & Steve would be delighted to hear from you, especially with your success stories after reading and applying the steps in this book.

They can be reached by...

Telephone: 702-259-9983

E-mail: Brenth2009@gmail.com

steve.hackney@academyforgrowth.co.uk

Mail: BHI Bookkeeping, Payroll & Income Tax
2385 N. Decatur Blvd.
Las Vegas, NV 89108

Notes

Notes

Notes

Notes

Notes

Notes

Notes

Notes

Notes

Notes